BIBLE DISCOVERERS

MOSES
AND THE
TEN COMMANDMENTS

RETOLD BY *Victoria Parker*
❖
CONSULTANT *Janet Dyson*

BIBLE DISCOVERERS

MOSES
AND THE
TEN COMMANDMENTS

CLASSIC STORIES FROM THE OLD TESTAMENT

RETOLD BY *Victoria Parker* ❖ CONSULTANT *Janet Dyson*

southwater

This edition is published by Southwater

Distributed in the UK by
The Manning Partnership
251–253 London Road East
Batheaston
Bath BA1 7RL
tel. 01225 852 727
fax 01225 852 852

Published in the USA by
Anness Publishing Inc.
27 West 20th Street
Suite 504
New York
NY 10011
fax 212 807 6813

Distributed in Canada by
General Publishing
895 Don Mills Road
400–402 Park Centre
Toronto, Ontario M3C 1W3
tel. 416 445 3333
fax 416 445 5991

Distributed in Australia by
Sandstone Publishing
Unit 1, 360 Norton Street
Leichhardt
New South Wales 2040
tel. 02 9560 7888
fax 02 9560 7488

Southwater is an imprint of Anness Publishing Limited
Hermes House, 88–89 Blackfriars Road, London SE1 8HA
tel. 020 7401 2077; fax 020 7633 9499

© Anness Publishing Limited 2000, 2002

Publisher: Joanna Lorenz
Managing Editor: Gilly Cameron Cooper
Senior Editor: Lisa Miles
Produced by Miles Kelly Publishing Limited
11 Bardfield Centre, Great Bardfield, Essex CM7 4SL
Editorial Director: Paula Borton
Art Director: Clare Sleven
Project Editor: Neil de Cort
Designer: Jill Mumford
Information author: Kamini Khanduri
Picture Research: Lesley Cartlidge and Liberty Mella
Copy Editor: Sarah Ridley
Editorial Reader: Joy Wotton
Indexing: Janet De Saulles
Design Consultant: Sarah Ponder
Education Consultant: Janet Dyson
Illustration: Galante Book Illustration

PHOTOGRAPHIC CREDITS
6 (B/L) Erich Lessing/ AKG London.
29 (B/L) The Stock Market.
30 (B/L) Erich Lessing/ AKG London.
32 (B/L) Jean-Léo Dugast/ AKG London.
41 (B/C) Erich Lessing/ AKG London.
42 (B/C) Erich Lessing/ AKG London.
47 (B/R) Erich Lessing/ AKG London.
48 (B/R) Erich Lessing/ AKG London.
All other images from the Miles Kelly Archive.
The Publishers would like to thank the following artists who
have contributed to this book:
Studio Galante (Virgil Pomfret Agency):
L.R. Galante   Manuela Cappon
Alessandro Menchi   Francesco Spadoni
                    Also:
Vanessa Card   Terry Riley   Shane Marsh
Rob Sheffield   Terry Gabbey   (Linden Artists)
Wayne Ford   Alison Winfield   Maps by
Sally Holmes   Neil Gower   Martin Sanders

Previously published as *Discovering the Bible: Samson and Delilah*

1 3 5 7 9 10 8 6 4 2

Contents

Introduction

THIS book covers the part of the Old Testament from halfway through Exodus to the end of Ruth. At the beginning of the book, the Israelites are a group of homeless wanderers in the desert, and by the end they have settled in the Promised Land. This book tells of their struggles along the way and charts the rises and falls of their faith in God.

The first story, "Manna from Heaven," describes the early years in the wilderness, when God provides manna and quails to feed His starving people. In "The First Battle," the Israelites experience their first victory in their campaign to take over the Promised Land. When they arrive at Mount Sinai, God tells Moses the laws by which He wants His people to live their lives, including the most important laws, known as the Ten Commandments. According to God's instructions, a holy tent called a tabernacle is built. This is to be God's home on earth, a visible sign that He is living among His people. The Israelites carry it with them until they settle in Canaan and set it up permanently.

On their leaving Mount Sinai, another period of wandering begins, and the Israelites grow weary of the months of hardship. When they finally reach the borders of Canaan, they are too afraid to obey God's order to attack the local people. God is so angry at their disobedience, he punishes them by sentencing them to another 40 years of wandering. As the years go by, the Israelites who had fled from Egypt grow older and die, and a new generation grows up. These young people have never known anything but the struggles of the traveling life and are better adapted than their parents were. They fight battle after battle with the local people, trying to drive them from their homes and take over their lands.

A long journey
The Exodus began in the fertile Nile valley, which must have made the hardships of the wilderness even harder to take.

Calm before the storm
Before the Israelites invaded the Promised Land, they camped here, at the Oasis of Jericho, near Gilgal, to rest.

The story "Death of Moses" tells of the great leader's last days. Although Moses does not enter the Promised Land, he climbs to the top of Mount Nebo to see with his own eyes the land his people will inherit. Before he dies, he hands over the leadership to his successor, Joshua. The following stories describe Joshua's impressive achievements as leader, from crossing the mighty river Jordan to storming the great city of Jericho. He goes on to capture the town of Ai, and he is tricked into making a treaty with the people of Gibeon. In the story "The Longest Day," he manages to overcome five of the region's kings in one long battle. At last, after many victories and much bloodshed, the Israelites finally take over the land of Canaan. The Promised Land is divided among the tribes, and the Israelites settle down to a life of farming and homemaking.

After the death of Joshua, no single leader takes over. Instead, the Israelites are ruled by a succession of Judges, including Deborah, Gideon, Jephthah, and Samson. Before the Judges begin to rule, there has been peace for many years. But as time goes by, people start to forget the struggles of the past and the hard-won victories. Instead of continuing to wage war on their enemies, as God had ordered, they begin to live alongside them as neighbors. Despite the Judges' warnings, they even start to worship the Canaanite gods. Time after time, God punishes his people by letting them fall into the hands of foreign rulers. After a period of suffering, they beg for forgiveness, and God appoints a Judge to save them. But as soon as the Judge dies, they slip back into their sinful ways.

Pilgrims to Jerusalem
A trip to the holy city of Jerusalem, first colonized by the Israelites at the time of Joshua, has been a goal for religious pilgrims like these for hundreds of years.

In contrast to all the discord in the stories of the Judges, the book ends with the story of Ruth—a gentle tale that deals with family life and everyday issues. Although it relates to the same period as the Judges, its subject matter is very different. The story ends with the birth of Ruth's baby, who will grow up to become the grandfather of the greatest King of Israel, David.

Throughout this book, the Israelites' faith in God ebbs and flows. After the Exodus from Egypt, their faith is strong, and they look forward with excitement to reaching the Promised Land. When thirst and hunger take over, though, their faith weakens until God provides food and water, and they win their first victory. God is well aware of the weaknesses of His people, and accepts a great deal of wrongdoing from them. The story of the Golden Calf is another low point, when the people turn from God and start to worship an idol. Their faith is reestablished with the building of the tabernacle. Once back on their travels, the Israelites become impatient again and begin to have doubts about Moses as their leader. When they disobey God's instruction to invade Canaan, their punishment is another 40 years of wandering. Although a period of strong faith follows the crossing of the Jordan, it ebbs away after Joshua's death. This book shows the remarkable faith and leadership of Moses, who continually defends his erring people against the wrath of God.

✦ **FROM EGYPT TO THE PROMISED LAND** ✦

This book covers the Israelites' time in the wilderness after the Exodus, their entry into the Promised Land, and settling down in their new country.

IN THE WILDERNESS
Exodus, Ch. 16–18.
Numbers, Ch. 11–22.
THE TEN COMMANDMENTS
Exodus, Ch. 19 & 20.
THE DEATH OF MOSES
Deuteronomy, Ch. 31–34.
ENTERING THE PROMISED LAND
Joshua, Ch. 1–4.
JOSHUA IN CANAAN
Joshua, Ch. 6–24.
THE TIME OF THE JUDGES
Judges, Ch. 1–17.
RUTH
Ruth, Ch. 1–4.

Holy mountain
Mount Sinai, which at the time of the Bible was called Mount Horeb, was already a holy place before God gave Moses the Ten Commandments there. It was where Moses was first spoken to by God from the burning bush, when he was told he was to lead the Israelites from slavery in Egypt. He was told by God to remove his sandals, a common sign of respect still followed in many places of worship today.

Egypt to the Promised Land

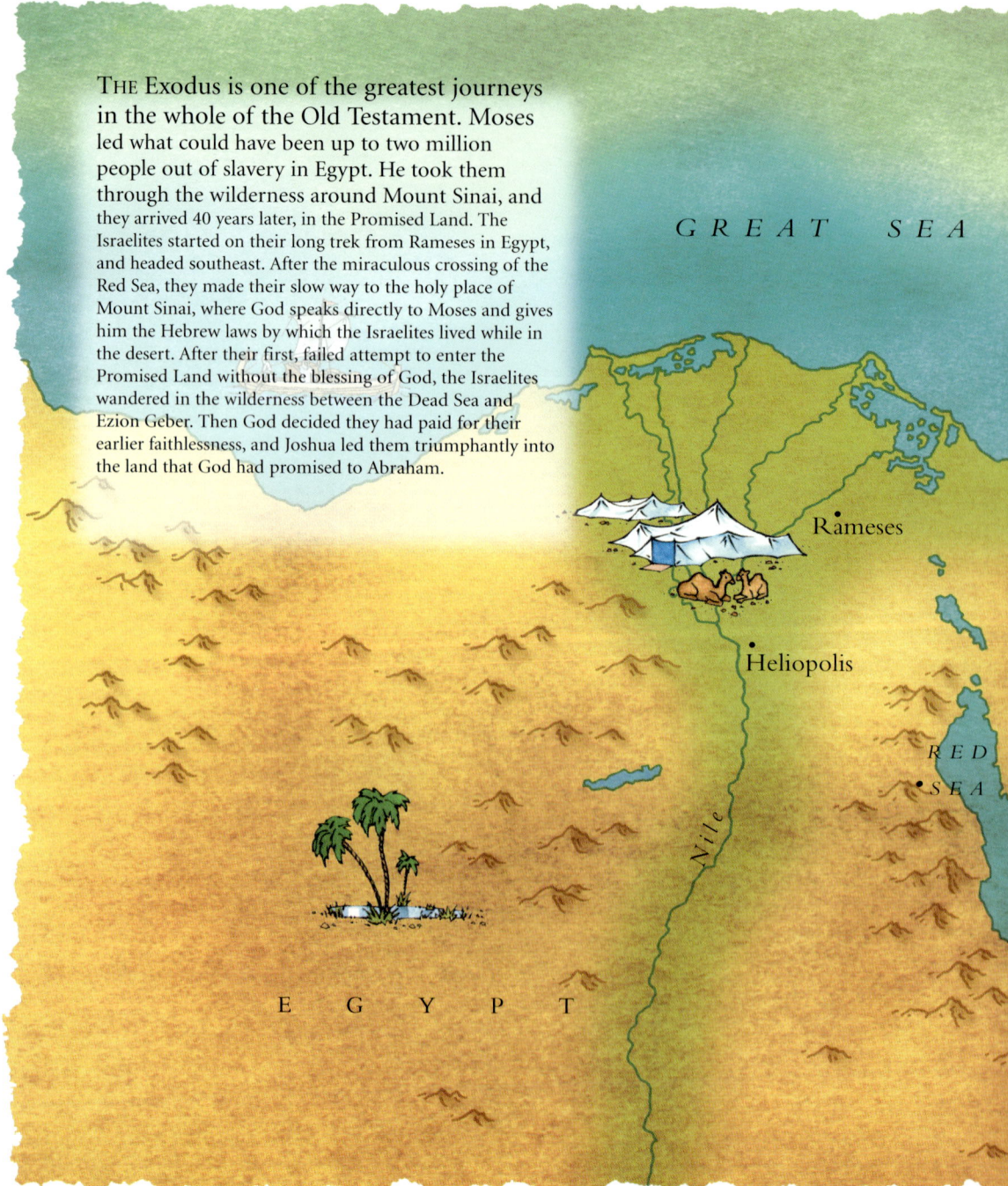

THE Exodus is one of the greatest journeys in the whole of the Old Testament. Moses led what could have been up to two million people out of slavery in Egypt. He took them through the wilderness around Mount Sinai, and they arrived 40 years later, in the Promised Land. The Israelites started on their long trek from Rameses in Egypt, and headed southeast. After the miraculous crossing of the Red Sea, they made their slow way to the holy place of Mount Sinai, where God speaks directly to Moses and gives him the Hebrew laws by which the Israelites lived while in the desert. After their first, failed attempt to enter the Promised Land without the blessing of God, the Israelites wandered in the wilderness between the Dead Sea and Ezion Geber. Then God decided they had paid for their earlier faithlessness, and Joshua led them triumphantly into the land that God had promised to Abraham.

GREAT   SEA

Rameses

Heliopolis

RED
SEA

Nile

E   G   Y   P   T

Hazor•

Shechem•

Bethel•
Jericho•

• Gaza

• Beersheba

• Ezion Geber

Mt.Sinai

M I D I A N

Manna from Heaven

JUST as God had promised centuries earlier, Abraham's descendants had now become a great people—the Israelite nation. The mighty Egyptian Pharaoh had done everything in his power to crush them but had been defeated, all thanks to the work of the Lord. For the first time in over four centuries, the Israelites were free, but homeless.

Imagine how tough it must have been for the hundreds of thousands of people who found themselves wandering through the Sinai Desert, not knowing where they were going or when they might get there. Mothers nursing their babies, children wailing with exhaustion and men weighed down by their family's belongings. Day after day they plodded on together with only the cold, uncomfortable nights and the occasional rest days of the Sabbath to mark time passing. The weeks seemed to melt together into an endless nightmare of heat, dust and walking . . . heat, dust and walking, and gradually their food began to run out. "We can't keep going like this!" some people moaned.

"We'd rather be back in Egypt," agreed others, feeling terribly hungry. "At least there we weren't starving."

God heard the suffering Israelites and called to Moses. "Reassure the people that I am with them," He said. "I shall make sure they don't go hungry."

Moses and Aaron gathered the famished people in a huge crowd. Aaron lifted his voice so his words of hope could be heard over the constant sound of crying, and the glory of the Lord suddenly came blazing through the clouds. Once again, Moses heard God speaking to him. Aaron announced the message. "Know that the Lord is with you," he thundered, as the people tried to shield themselves from the blinding light. "Today, He will give you meat to eat, and tomorrow, He shall bring you bread!"

In the evening, as dusk fell, flocks of quails appeared in the sky and fluttered down to land around the camp. The starving Israelites dashed eagerly back and forth catching the little birds, then settled down to a feast of roasted

> " *Then the Lord said to Moses, 'Behold, I will rain bread from Heaven for you.'* "

quail. That night, for the first time in weeks and weeks, they slept without the nagging ache of hunger interrupting their dreams.

Next morning, the Hebrews awoke to find strange, round, white flakes covering the ground. At first, they thought it was frost. But on closer inspection, they were amazed to discover that it was a type of bread that tasted of honey. "We'll call it manna," they cried excitedly, "which means bread from the Lord!" They rushed to gather as much as they could, but a stern order from Moses stopped them. "The bread is a gift from God. Take only as much as you need for today," he warned. Some people didn't listen and secretly hoarded manna in their tents. But they soon came to regret it when next day they found that the manna had turned moldy. They also realized that there was no need to have saved it, for once again, there was fresh manna everywhere.

The manna appeared for six days and on the morning before the Sabbath, Moses told the people to gather twice as much. "There will be no manna tomorrow," Moses explained, "so we can spend the day worshiping God and resting, as is proper." When the Sabbath dawned, they found that the manna they had kept overnight was just as delicious as before. But once again, there were some who disobeyed. They went out looking for more. When the Lord saw these groups of greedy people, He was very disappointed. "How long will the people ignore my wishes?" He said to Moses. Yet He kept sending the manna day after day, to feed the hungry Israelites.

It wasn't long, however, before the Israelites were again complaining. When they reached Rephidim, they set up camp, but there was no water to be found.

"If we keep following Moses and Aaron through this wilderness, we'll surely die of thirst," the people gasped angrily. "Tell God to send us water—or else!" they croaked through cracked lips at Moses and Aaron.

When the Lord heard the people's challenge, He was again deeply saddened. But even so, He still didn't desert them. He instructed Moses to strike a rock with his crook. As the rock split apart with an almighty crack, a jet of icy water came gushing through, creating a waterfall from which everyone could quench their thirst.

A flock of quails
A quail is a small, brown, short-tailed bird, like a tiny pheasant. Quails cross the Sinai Peninsula on their migrations between Europe and Africa. They can fly quickly for short periods of time but get tired on longer journeys. When this happens, they fly very slowly and very low which makes them easy to catch.

Daily bread
During their 40 years in the wilderness, the Israelites relied on the manna for food. The only time it would last overnight was the day before the Sabbath, the only time that God said they should collect more than they could eat in a day. This shows how in control God was and how reliant the Israelites were on Him.

What is manna?
The word "manna" means "What is it?" in Hebrew. In the Bible, manna is described as white, like coriander seeds, and tasting like wafers made with honey. It is not known exactly what this substance is. Some people believe it is a sweet, white substance produced by some desert plants, such as the hammada shrub (see right). However, the regular appearance of the manna on six days out of seven, and the amount of it, point to God carrying out His will by controlling natural events.

The First Battle

IN every area the Israelites traveled through, they made the local people very nervous. Imagine how intimidating it would be if you lived in a small desert community, and suddenly more than 600,000 people looking for a home arrived on your doorstep—people you knew had defeated the mighty Egyptian army! The Israelites must have expected trouble to brew up sooner or later, and it first happened while they were camped at Rephidim. The leader of a local tribe, a man named Amalek, came to meet Moses, challenging the Israelites and declaring war.

Even though there were a lot of Israelites, they weren't at all ready to go out and fight. They had been traveling through the desert for many months and had little remaining strength to attack an enemy. But, unfortunately, they also had no choice. Moses considered all the people and entrusted the courageous young Joshua with the job of somehow turning the weary Israelites into fierce soldiers. "I want you to choose men for our troops and lead them in the battle against Amalek tomorrow," Moses told him. "Don't be afraid! God will be with us."

The next day, Aaron and Hur accompanied Moses to the top of a nearby hill. With pounding hearts they watched as Joshua and the Israelites raced out to meet the savage Amalekites and clashed into a seething tangle of blood and determination. Praying to the Lord, Moses took his crook and lifted up his arms to Heaven. Almost immediately, Aaron and Hur noticed that the Israelites began to have the upper hand. In the midst of all the slashing and stabbing, they could see Amalekites dropping on every side. But it wasn't to last. Moses gradually grew tired, and when he could hold his shaking arms up no longer, the tide suddenly

> **❝ *Joshua mowed down Amalek and his people with the edge of the sword.* ❞**

turned. Suddenly it seemed as if there were Amalekites everywhere, killing Israelites whichever way Aaron and Hur looked. In desperation, the two men moved a rock so Moses could sit on it and then took up position on either side, each holding up one of Moses's hands. All day, Aaron and Hur supported Moses without wavering. No matter how cold or weary their muscles became, they kept his arms aloft. And when the sun finally set, they heard cheering. The Israelites had won their first battle!

Now rumors had already spread of how God had brought the Israelites out of slavery and defeated the Egyptian army. And when news of this most recent victory reached Jethro, Moses's father-in-law, he rushed to be with Moses and join in the celebrations. Jethro knew that his son-in-law had become a great leader, but even so, he was surprised to see how the people relied on Moses to decide everything for them. Jethro found Moses surrounded by huge crowds, everyone wanting private guidance from God and a solution to their individual problems. The people thought nothing of waiting around all day in the hope of talking to Moses. Jethro was shocked. "This is no good!" he told his son-in-law. "You'll soon be exhausted, and the people will never get anything done. The nation has grown too big for you to manage on your own. Divide the people into groups, appointing a good man at the head of each one. Choose leaders you can trust to make their own decisions on everyday matters, while you deal with the more important issues, making sure that God's will is being done." So Moses set wise judges as governors over the people and arranged the Israelites into a strong nation under his command and the leadership of the Lord.

Joshua

This story contains the first mention of Joshua, when Moses chooses him as his assistant. Joshua achieves victory in this first battle. Later, when the Israelites reach the border of Canaan, he and another man, named Caleb, are the only ones who trust God's judgment and are prepared to invade when God tells them to. Because of this, only Joshua and Caleb of the original Israelites actually enter Canaan. Joshua, like Moses, has patience and humility, and he goes on to succeed Moses as leader of the Israelites and to fight many successful campaigns in Canaan.

❧ ABOUT THE STORY ❧

Joshua is given the difficult task of organizing the Israelites into an army to fight the Amalekites. During the battle, Moses raises his crook to Heaven in prayer. As long as he holds up his arms, God is on the Israelites' side, but whenever he lowers them, the Amalekites fight back. At sunset, God brings the Israelites victory. Moses then appoints judges to rule over the people. He is now free to deal with the most important matters.

The Ten Commandments

THREE months after they had left Egypt, the Israelites reached a mountain called Mount Sinai and made camp there. This peak, which thrust up toward heaven itself and towered over the wilderness all around, was believed to be a holy place, and Moses climbed to the top to talk to the Lord alone.

"The people have seen what I did to the Egyptians for their sake; they have seen how I lifted them out of slavery and have been with them ever since, looking after them on their wanderings," said the Lord. "All the earth is mine—and if the Israelites are true to me and my wishes, I shall make them a holy nation. Tell the people to prepare themselves," God ordered Moses, "for in three days' time, I shall come down to Mount Sinai myself to give you my sacred laws. All the people will be able to see me descend from heaven, but you must put up barriers around the foot of the mountain so no one sets foot on this holy ground. If anyone disobeys, they will die."

> 66 *And Moses went up to God, and the Lord called to him out of the mountain.* 99

On the morning of the third day, spears of lightning suddenly started to stab through the clouds, and giant drumrolls of thunder came rumbling over the people's heads, threatening to bring the heavens tumbling down on top of them. While the Israelites stood gazing upward like fearful statues, the skies split open with a mighty blast of trumpets and flames came bursting through, consuming the peak in fire. The ground began to tremble and quake as Mount Sinai was turned into a blazing torch, and the people tried to shield themselves from the searing light and burning heat. Above them, the smoke gathered in a heavy cloud, which spread a shadow all around and darkened their faces. And when the thick fog had completely wrapped the mountaintop from their view, all eyes turned to the small figures of Moses and Aaron making their way up the slopes. Closer and closer the two men drew to the dense, smoldering cloud, then—without hesitating—they walked straight into it.

God spoke to Moses on the mountain top, telling him all the laws for His people to obey, but ten were the most important:

You must not have any other God except me.

You must not make and worship statues or pictures of anything in the skies, on earth or in the sea.

Mount Sinai
It is not known exactly where Mount Sinai is, but it is usually identified as a mountain called Jebel Musa (above). God appeared to Moses on Mount Sinai, also known as Mount Horeb, and gave him the Ten Commandments.

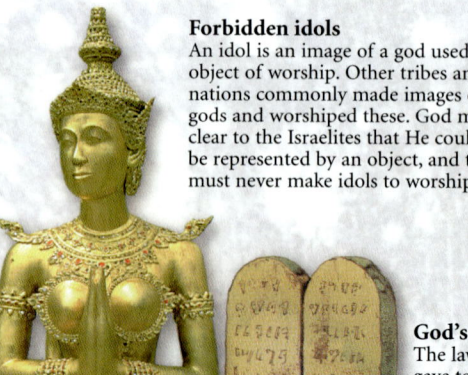

Forbidden idols
An idol is an image of a god used as an object of worship. Other tribes and nations commonly made images of their gods and worshiped these. God made it clear to the Israelites that He could never be represented by an object, and that they must never make idols to worship.

God's contract
The laws God gave to Moses would be carved onto two stone tablets as a contract between God and His people.

You must use the Lord's name only in a respectful way.

You must keep the Sabbath, the seventh day of the week, as a holy day of rest and worship.

You must love your father and mother.

You must not kill anyone.

You must not love anyone else's husband or wife.

You must not steal.

You must not lie.

You must not envy other people's possessions.

Meanwhile, at the foot of the mountain, the Israelites were terrified. The smoke pouring out above them was thicker than ever, lightning was whipcracking across the clouds, and above the raging of the thunderstorm could be heard the blaring of almighty trumpets. How relieved the people were when they saw Moses and Aaron coming down from the mountain and when they saw even more amazingly that they were completely unharmed! But they were no less terrified by God's power.

"Don't be so afraid," Moses told them. "God has chosen to appear to you like this so you'll never forget who He is and what He wants of you."

"We'll do everything the Lord says," everyone agreed, and that night Moses wrote down every word God had spoken in a book of laws, which the Israelites would keep, to make sure they remembered God's commands.

Early next morning, Moses set about building a huge altar at the foot of the mountain. All the people gathered in front of it, impatient to find out what God had said. Then the whole crowd listened in silence as Moses read his book of laws aloud. When he had finished, the nation solemnly swore to obey the Lord's words.

YOU SHALL HAVE NO OTHER GODS BEFORE ME.

❋

YOU SHALL NOT MAKE FOR YOURSELF A GRAVEN IMAGE, OR ANY LIKENESS OF ANYTHING THAT IS IN HEAVEN ABOVE OR THAT IS IN THE EARTH BENEATH OR THAT IS IN THE WATER UNDER THE EARTH.

❋

YOU SHALL NOT TAKE THE NAME OF THE LORD YOUR GOD IN VAIN.

❋

REMEMBER THE SABBATH DAY, TO KEEP IT HOLY.

HONOR YOUR FATHER AND YOUR MOTHER.

❋

YOU SHALL NOT KILL.

❋

YOU SHALL NOT COMMIT ADULTERY.

❋

YOU SHALL NOT STEAL.

❋

YOU SHALL NOT BEAR FALSE WITNESS.

❋

YOU SHALL NOT COVET YOUR NEIGHBOR'S HOUSE.

❋

❧ ABOUT THE STORY ❧

In this story, God comes down from heaven to reveal His sacred laws. The people watch in amazement as Moses and Aaron disappear up the mountain to hear the laws. The most important laws are the Ten Commandments—the ten basic rules by which God wants His people to live their lives from now on. The Ten Commandments and the other laws form God's covenant with His people.

The Golden Calf

GOD summoned Moses again to the top of Mount Sinai, this time without Aaron. The Israelites watched nervously as Moses ventured into the darkness of the low, hovering cloud all by himself and disappeared from view. The people were eager for God to talk to them once more, and they kept a vigil at the foot of the mountain. But days passed into weeks without any sign of Moses, and the Israelites started to get impatient. "Where is Moses?" they wondered, tired with waiting. "Whatever is he doing?"

"He can't be talking to God all this time!" some said.

"He's abandoned us!" cried others, angrily.

"Tell us what to do!" the people shouted, surging forward. "Give us a new god to follow!"

Aaron could see he had a riot on his hands and he was very worried. Thinking quickly, he ordered everyone to take off their gold jewelry and bring it to him. Soon a heap of glittering treasure was piled at his feet, and after melting it down, Aaron made the gold into the likeness of a calf. All the time Aaron was working he could hear the people growing out of control, and he hurried to build an altar too. "Here is your new god," he roared, taking the dull-eyed monster to show them. To his relief the people were delighted, and he declared a feast day to the new god.

At the top of the mountain, God looked down at the Israelite camp and was beside Himself with wrath. "I am furious with these unfaithful people," He thundered. "I will destroy them all!" But Moses begged the Lord to be merciful and managed to persuade the Lord to leave punishing the people to him. Moses hurried off down the

mountain, carefully carrying two stone tablets on which the Lord had written the laws by His very own hand.

Long before he reached the camp, the angry Moses could hear the wild noise of celebrating. When he finally caught sight of the Israelites he was enraged and slammed the stone tablets to the ground, where they shattered into a million pieces. He seized the idol and burned it, before grinding it down into razor-sharp grains which he threw into the Israelites' water and made them drink.

"Don't blame me!" cried Aaron. "You know how sinful the people can be! I just collected their gold jewelry, threw it into the fire, and out came this golden calf all by itself!" he lied, daringly.

Apis the Bull
This picture shows the Egyptian god Apis the Bull. The golden calf made by Aaron may have been modeled on Apis; as the Israelites had lived in Egypt, they knew about bull worship. In Egypt, the bull or calf was a symbol of fertility and strength.

The Levites
The Levites in the story were members of the tribe of Levi, which was Moses' own tribe. They were God's faithful followers, who helped Moses to punish the sinful Israelites. The Levites later became the assistants of the priests of the tabernacle. The picture shows the Levites slaying the Israelites.

When Moses realized that even his own brother's heart had become evil, he stood in the gateway of the camp, blocking anyone from leaving. "Who is on the side of the Lord?" he demanded of the whole nation. "If anyone remains faithful to God, come and stand by me." Right away, members of Moses' own tribe of Levi pushed their way through to Moses. His eyes were cold, and his voice was stern and unforgiving. "Now put on your swords and slay all the unbelievers," he instructed the Levites. Moses didn't speak again until nearly 3,000 people lay dead. "You have sinned a great sin," he admonished the grief-stricken Israelites. "I will speak to the Lord, to see if I can somehow make up for it."

> **Moses's anger burned hot, and he threw down the tablets and broke them.**

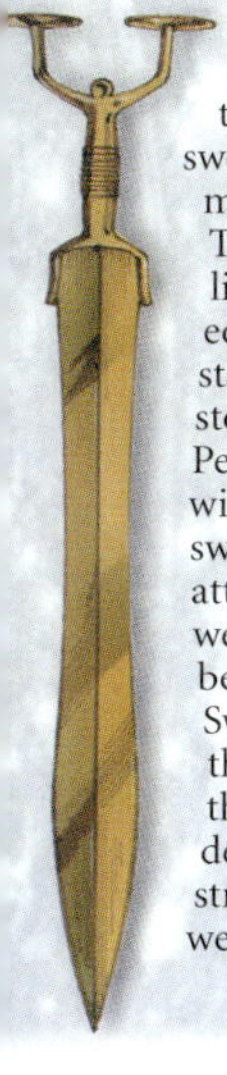

Once more God forgave the Israelites their faithlessness and renewed His covenant with them. He also again wrote the laws by hand on two stone tablets. "Now go and lead my people to the Promised Land," He told Moses. "I will send my angel to lead the way. But the people have today sinned greatly against me and I shall not forget it."

Swords
The Levites used swords to kill the unfaithful Israelites. The sword is the most frequently mentioned weapon in the Bible. The earliest swords were usually like daggers—straight, double-edged, and used mainly for stabbing. By the time of this story the Philistines, the Sea People, had introduced swords with longer blades. These swords were kept in a sheath attached to a belt when they were not in use, and they became more and more popular. Swords have been found all over the Middle East, and many of the sword hilts were very richly decorated, often with symbols of strength, like lions, to help the wearer in battle.

Gold
Some of the Israelites would have learned metalworking while in Egypt, so they could have helped Aaron make the golden calf. They could also have made the kind of gold jewelry shown here— rings, bracelets and nose-rings — that was worn by women at the time.

∽ ABOUT THE STORY ∽

Impatient for Moses to reappear, the Israelites begin to lose faith in God, begging Aaron to find them another god. Aaron makes the golden calf, which he presents to them as their new god. God is furious and ready to destroy them. However, Moses intervenes. Only the faithful Levites stand by Moses and carry out God's punishment. God then forgives his people and renews his covenant with them.

The Tabernacle

MOSES gathered all the people of Israel together and said, "The time is close at hand when we must leave Mount Sinai. However, before we move on to the Promised Land of Canaan, there is one very important thing God has asked of us that we must do. We must build Him a tabernacle—a holy tent where we can meet and pray—and a sacred chest called an ark to keep safe the stone tablets of His law. Anyone who would like to contribute toward these things is welcome to give materials, and any offers of help to do the building will be gratefully received."

The people went back to their tents very excited. What an honor it was to have the responsibility of making these things for the Lord Himself! Everyone began searching through their belongings, all eager to provide their most prized possessions to make the tabernacle and ark as splendid as possible.

Soon people all over the camp were flooding toward Moses' tent to offer their treasures. They gave their jewelry, ornaments, and dishes of silver and bronze; sweet-smelling acacia wood; rich materials, and the very best linen and animal skins. The leaders of the tribes offered precious gemstones and exotic spices and oils. Everyone was so happy to be able to offer things to God!

Moses soon had more treasure than could be used and had to order the Israelites to stop coming with their gifts. Then he appointed expert craftsmen to take charge of the building, and the work started. Bit by bit, with great care, the Israelites constructed everything according to the design that God Himself had given Moses on Mount

Sinai. There was to be an outer enclosure with the tabernacle inside, housing the ark itself. They also needed holy robes for Aaron, whom God had chosen as the High Priest, and for his sons, the priests who would serve the Lord inside the tabernacle. Everyone did their absolute best, for each person knew that only perfection would do.

Finally, the time came when everything was ready. Moses waited until the first day of the first month, just as God had ordered, and then painstakingly assembled everything. First, Moses set up the tabernacle itself. It had wooden walls, but looked from the outside like a grand tent because it was covered over on three sides from roof to floor. On the outside was strong weatherproof leather.

❧ ABOUT THE STORY ❧

The word "tabernacle" comes from the Latin "tabernaculum," meaning "tent." The significance of the tabernacle is that it shows God coming to live with His people. He sets up His tent among their tents. The tabernacle is a confirmation that God has forgiven His people for their past sins. The Israelites carry it with them on their journey and are reassured to know that God is traveling with them.

Sacred lamps
The type of seven-armed lamp-stand that Moses set up in the Holy Place is called a "menorah." It had a main stem, with three branches protruding from either side of this. The main stem supported a lampholder, and each branch ended in a flower-shaped lampholder. The whole lamp-stand was made of gold.

Trees in the desert
The ark was made from acacia wood, for the acacia was one of the few trees that would have grown in the desert. Acacia trees still grow in dry parts of the world today.

Moses set the entrance to the tabernacle at the eastern end, through a curtain hanging from five pillars. Then he prepared the inside. All around the ceiling and walls, Moses hung linen curtains in a wonderful blaze of violet, purple and scarlet. Then, just as God had instructed, Moses hung up a curtain called the Veil to divide the tabernacle into two rooms. The innermost room was called the Holy of Holies, and it was here that Moses positioned the ark of the covenant . Inside the sacred chest he laid the holy stone tablets on which God had written the Law. Then Moses sealed the lid. Returning back outside the Holy of Holies, Moses then set an altar in front of the Veil. He ordered the priests to keep incense burning there day and night, so beautiful-smelling smoke would waft up, accompanying their prayers to Heaven. Then Moses set up the second room inside the tabernacle, the Holy Place, with a seven-armed lamp-stand and a table holding 12 sacred loaves, each representing one of the 12 tribes. Going outside the tabernacle, Moses positioned the priests' washbasin, and filled it with water, then Aaron and his sons purified themselves with cleansing rituals. Next Moses set up the Altar of Burnt Offering and made the very first of the daily sacrifices that were to take place there. Finally, Moses put up the enclosure wall, to screen everything from view.

When Moses's work was finished, everyone saw a cloud descend over the tabernacle and a light enter the Holy of Holies—so bright that not even Moses could enter there. From that moment onward, the Israelites moved off on their travels only when God gave the sign by lifting the cloud from the tabernacle.

66 *The people of Israel had done all the work, and Moses blessed them.* 99

The Ark of the Covenant
The word "ark" comes from the Latin word *arca*, which means "chest." The ark was a rectangular wooden box, decorated with gold. On the lid were two cherubs with outspread wings, between which God was supposed to live when on earth. The ark could be carried by inserting poles through gold rings attached to its sides. It was known by various names, including "The Ark of the Covenant" and "The Ark of the Lord." The two tablets inscribed with the Ten Commandments were kept inside the ark.

Holy robes
This picture shows the clothes that Aaron wore as the high priest of the tabernacle. Bells and pomegranates hung in a fringe from the hem of his long robe, and the shorter tunic over the top was tied with a girdle. His breastplate was decorated with 12 precious stones, one for each of the 12 tribes of Israel.

In the Wilderness

AT God's command, the Israelites left Mount Sinai and set out on the final stages of their journey toward Canaan. The Lord had sent so many signs to prove He was with them that the people should have forged ahead with confidence. But as the months of hardship went on, their faith wavered once again. Eventually, even Aaron and Miriam, Moses's own family, became discontented. "Who does Moses think he is? After all, he's not the only one God has appeared to!" The Lord was furious and summoned them to the tabernacle. "How dare you!" He roared. "I may sometimes talk to people in a dream, but Moses sees me as I am and talks to me face to face!" Miriam hung her head in shame and was horrified to see that her hands were covered with the sores of leprosy! She was cast out of the camp at once and left to suffer in the wilderness. Aaron knew that Miriam's only hope was for Moses to ask the Lord for mercy. Aaron begged Moses for help, and a week later Miriam found herself healed.

The miserable rabble eventually reached Canaan. However, several tribes were already settled in the country, people who would fight to defend their homes. So God instructed Moses to send 12 men to check out the land. After 40 days they returned with wonderful reports of how beautiful and fertile the countryside was. But they also warned that the local tribes would be hard to conquer, and spread fear with stories of giant men and earthquakes. Only Joshua and Caleb trusted that it was the right time to attack. But the scared Israelites would not follow them.

> " The Lord said to Moses,
> 'How long will this people
> despise me?' "

The Lord was furious. "How long will you people go on refusing to believe what I say?" He thundered in the tabernacle. "Because you have turned your backs on the country I promised you, I shall give Canaan to your children instead. You will be condemned to wander for 40 years. You will die homeless, and your bodies will rot here in this wilderness, all except Joshua and Caleb!" At this threat, the Israelites grew desperate. Many of them rushed out early the next morning to begin an attack. But without God's blessing, the raiders were all killed. And in the camp, all the spies that told lies about Canaan were found dead of a mysterious disease.

With the hope of entering the Promised Land now gone, the Israelites felt they had nothing left to lose. They thought Moses had lured them away from their homes for nothing but an empty promise. They no longer respected his leadership and began to rise up against him. When three ringleaders named Korah, Dathan and Abiram, demanded that they and 247 other men be allowed to be priests, Moses decided he'd had enough. "Do what you like with them, Lord!" he cried. Next day, in front of all those gathered to worship, Moses announced, "These men want to be priests. It is against God's wishes, but I am powerless to stop them." As he finished speaking, there was a resounding crack, and the ground swallowed up the would-be priests, their families and all their belongings.

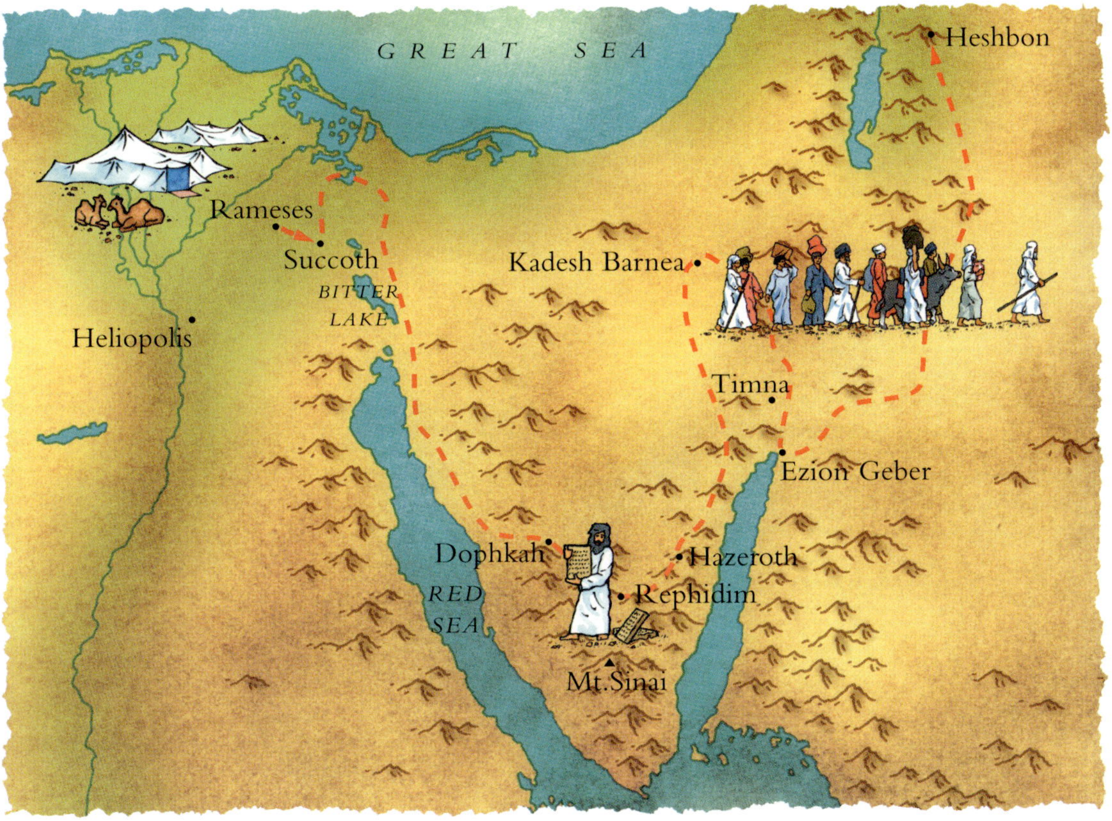

Heshbon

GREAT SEA

Rameses

Succoth

Heliopolis

BITTER
LAKE

Kadesh Barnea

Timna

Ezion Geber

Dophkah

RED
SEA

Hazeroth

Rephidim

Mt.Sinai

To end the peoples' uprisings once and for all, the Lord told Moses to instruct each tribe to bring him a rod with their leader's name written on it. When Moses put all the rods in the tabernacle, everyone was amazed to see that Aaron's blossomed with flowers and budded into almonds. Everyone was warned by this sign that Aaron was God's chosen High Priest, and Moses kept the rod as a reminder to everyone not to question God's will again.

The Exodus from Egypt
After the miraculous crossing of the Red Sea, the Israelites still had a long way to go to reach the Promised Land. They first made their way through the wilderness by the Bitter Lake. At Rephidim Moses performed the miracle of getting water from the rock for the Israelites. Then the Israelites camped at Sinai, and Moses received the Ten Commandments from God. At Kadesh Barnea Moses sent out the spies whose false report condemned the Israelites to 40 years' wandering in the desert.

A great leader
Despite the Israelites' lack of faith, Moses remains loyal to his people, constantly appealing to God for mercy on their behalf. God himself pays tribute to Moses, telling Miriam and Aaron that He singles out Moses by appearing to him face to face, rather than in a dream or vision (Numbers 12: 6–8). Moses never seeks power for himself, and he is happy to spend his life carrying out God's will.

A sign from God
To try to end the problems of the Israelites, God sent a sign, a blossoming almond branch, to show them all that Aaron was His chosen priest.

⋆ **ABOUT THE STORY** ⋆

Once again, the Israelites begin to doubt Moses's word. God is furious at their contempt for Moses. When the people refuse to obey Him and invade the cities of Canaan, God's punishment is severe; He sentences them to another 40 years in the wilderness.

Balak and Balaam

THE years of wandering continued, and the Israelites who had disobeyed God began to age and die—Miriam and Aaron among them—just as the Lord had vowed they would. A new generation began to grow up to take their place: tough young people who had never known anything but the hardships of the traveling life and who were well trained in fighting skills. As the nation moved around the borders of Canaan, the local tribes came out to defend their homes, and though sometimes the Israelites were forced back by the sheer number of warriors facing them, on many occasions they engaged in fierce battles. With the help of the Lord they began to win victory after victory, slaying the Amorite kings, Sihon of Heshbon and Og of Bashan, and taking their lands. Then they moved on into the plains of Moab.

The Moabites had heard of the destruction of the Amorite peoples, and when they saw the Israelites heading in their own direction, they were very frightened. Balak, the son of the king, decided there was nothing to do but to ask a great prophet named Balaam for help. Hastily, he sent several courtiers off to Balaam with money and an urgent message: "These Israelites we face won their way out of slavery in Egypt. How can we take on such a mighty people and win? Please come to Moab and put a curse on them, so we'll be able to drive them out of our lands."

Balaam listened to the courtiers and told them that he would answer their request for help the following morning, once he'd given it careful consideration. But that night, God appeared to him in his dreams. "Do not grant these people what they ask," He instructed Balaam, "for I have blessed the Israelite nation." Next day, the courtiers' faces fell as Balaam told them of his decision, and their hearts were heavy as they hurried back.

When Balak heard the disappointing news he began to panic, and instantly despatched some of his most highly regarded nobles—laden down with even more riches—to Balaam. "Balak will give you whatever you want," they begged the wise man. "Only please, we beg you, return with us to Moab and put a curse on the Israelites." Balaam felt very sorry for the desperate nobles. However, he still refused to help. "Even if Balak gave me his whole treasure-house, I couldn't go against the word of God," he explained. But during the night God spoke to him once again. "I shall allow you to go with the Moabites after all," He told Balaam, "but do only what I tell you to do."

When they woke up the next morning, the nobles were overjoyed to see Balaam saddling up his donkey. "There's no time to lose!" they cried, full of renewed hope, and they

> 66 *'The word that God puts in my mouth, that must I speak.'* 99

Telling the future
Balaam was a diviner, someone who tries to tell the future by magic. Several different forms of divination are mentioned in the Bible. One of these is astrology. Astrologers use the position of the sun, moon, planets and some of the constellations to predict the future. Unlike other forms of divination, astrology was not actually forbidden by Moses' law, but people did look down on it. They did not see it as a real science in the same way that they did astronomy, which involves studying the movements of the stars and planets.

hurried him off at once on the road back to Moab. Unfortunately, before they had gone very far, Balaam's donkey started to act up. She suddenly veered off the road and charged into a field, with the prophet clinging on for dear life. After heaving on the donkey's harness with all his strength, Balaam finally managed to bring her to a halt. As soon as he'd gotten his breath back, the angry prophet struck the animal with his staff.

After walking on a little way, the donkey suddenly shied again, this time crushing Balaam up against a wall and bruising his leg. The prophet was amazed that his usually peaceful animal was behaving in this way and once again dismounted to give the donkey a beating.

Imagine Balaam's dismay when, before they had got much farther down the road, he felt the donkey's legs begin to buckle beneath him. He managed to jump off just in time before the animal rolled over and lay down. "That's it!" yelled Balaam in anger, and he began to hit the donkey even more savagely than before.

Unbeknown to Balaam and the others, the donkey had taken fright three times because on each occasion the Angel of the Lord had suddenly appeared in front of her, blocking the way. Now, the poor animal was startled once again to find that she could talk! "What have I done?" she brayed at Balaam. "Why are you punishing me? I've never let you down before!"

Balaam was stunned, but he still managed to stutter a reply. "You made a fool of me, you stupid animal!" As soon as the words had left his lips, God lifted the veil that had been clouding the prophet's eyes and he saw the Angel of the Lord standing in front of him, brandishing his sword of flame. Balaam at once fell on his knees before the terrifying angel and prayed to God.

"I have sinned! But I didn't know the donkey was swerving to avoid you," he cried. "Have you come to tell me that I shouldn't be going to Moab? If so, I'll turn back right away."

"You may go and meet Balak, but be careful to say only what I tell you to say," the angel warned, sternly. Then he vanished, and the baffled men continued on their way.

Balak couldn't wait for the prophet to arrive at his palace, but rushed out to meet him instead. Wasting no time, he took Balaam up into the mountains, from where they could see all the tribes of Israel camped below. Three times, on three different peaks, Balak made a sacrifice to the Lord. And each time, on each peak, Balaam heard God telling him not to curse the Israelites, but to bless them. "Israel shall crush the people of Moab," Balaam prophesied. "The descendants of Jacob shall invade your cities and destroy them!" Needless to say, Balak was furious. He banished Balaam straight back home without delay. But everything came to pass just as Balaam had foretold, and the Israelites crushed the peoples of the plains of Moab.

Throwing arrows
Another way that people like Balaam may have tried to tell the future was through the practice of rhabdomancy. To do this, they would have taken a group of sticks or arrows, like those shown here, and thrown them into the air. Depending on how they landed they believed they could tell the future. Divination was widely practiced, but it was forbidden by God through Moses.

Balaam's donkey
In ancient times, donkeys were very important to poor people. They were the main form of transportation and could travel nearly 20 miles a day.

Death of Moses

WHEN Moses reached the age of 120 years, the Lord told him it was his time to die. It must have been bitterly disappointing for Moses, after all he had done to free the Israelites from slavery and guide them safely through the wilderness, that he would not live to enter the Promised Land. Yet over and above his sadness, he longed to take his place in heaven and be with God forever.

Summoning up his dwindling strength, Moses called the nation to gather together so he could speak to them for the last time. Moses looked out over the sea of faces, all anxiously looking up at him, to hear what he had to say. "The Lord has told me that I will not be going over the River Jordan with you," Moses told them.

The massive crowd gasped with one voice. They were deeply shocked. How would they manage to invade Canaan without Moses to tell them how? And whoever would be able to replace God's right-hand man?

Moses motioned for the people to calm down, and, when the noise from the crowd had died away, he raised his voice once again. "When the time comes to enter the Promised Land, the Lord Himself will go before you, destroying the people in your path. He will not let you down or abandon you, but will be with you always, leading you to victory."

Then Moses summoned Joshua to come and stand beside him, where all the people could see him. "Here is your new leader," Moses announced. "God has commanded that you shall follow Joshua!" A cheer rose up from the

⚜ ABOUT THE STORY ⚜

Moses was already 80 years old when he left Egypt. He spent the last 40 years of his life wandering in the wilderness. The length of time taken to reach the Promised Land was God's punishment to the Israelites for their lack of faith. Moses' faith remained strong, despite the fact that he was not to enter the land that was promised to his ancestors. The people's mourning was a tribute to Moses' greatness.

Mourning a death
When the Israelites were in mourning, they had certain rituals to perform. They might have removed their sandals, left their hair unbrushed or covered their heads with their hands. At funerals, people would hire mourners, like the Egyptian ones shown here, to make a better show at the burial.

Burial place
No one knows exactly where Moses was buried. Some people believe that the church on Mount Nebo, shown below, was built where his grave is situated.

front of the crowd and rippled backward through the people like a wave, and Moses turned to rest his trembling hands on the young man's broad shoulders. "Be strong and courageous, Joshua," he bade him. "For the day will come when you will lead these people triumphantly into the land that the Lord promised their fathers. Trust in God, and He will be with you in whatever you do."

> ❝ *'The Lord will be with you, He will not fail you, do not be afraid.'* ❞

Moses was worried that, once he had gone, the people would forget everything he'd told them and turn to wickedness. So he wrote down each word of all the laws that God had given him and entrusted them to the safe-keeping of the priests of the ark, so they could make sure that all the Israelites knew and understood them. Next, he went with Joshua to the tabernacle, to present the new leader of the people to the Lord. Finally, Moses called the elders of all the tribes together and gave them his blessing.

When all Moses' preparations were at last done, he went on his own to the top of Mount Pisgah.

"Look all around you," said the Lord, showing Moses the beautiful countryside of Canaan stretching away into the distance. "This is the land I promised to Abraham, Isaac and Jacob. Although you will not enter it yourself, I vow that it will belong to your descendants."

Moses died content that he had seen Canaan with his own eyes and with faith that it would indeed one day be his people's home. The whole Israelite nation had witnessed Moses' mighty power and great deeds, and they mourned his passing bitterly for 30 days.

MOSES WAS A GREAT MAN. ALTHOUGH HE WAS 120 YEARS OLD WHEN HE DIED, ACCORDING TO THE BIBLE, "HIS EYES WERE NOT DIM, NOR HIS NATURAL FORCE ABATED." ❧

Hebrew laws
The first five books of the Old Testament contain the Hebrew laws, also known as the Law of Moses. These are God's instructions to His people as to how they must live their lives. The most important laws are the Ten Commandments, but there are others on a wide range of subjects, such as how to keep healthy and punishments for lots of different crimes.

Moses' punishment
Many years earlier, Moses had once disobeyed God. His punishment was that he would not enter the Promised Land but only look upon it. This view shows Canaan over the sea of Galilee as Moses may have seen it before his death.

Rahab and the Spies

NOW that Moses was gone, the responsibility of rousing the Israelites to take the Promised Land rested squarely on Joshua's shoulders. But even though this was a daunting task, Joshua was not afraid. God spoke to him, inspiring him with confidence and courage. "It is time for you to lead the Israelites across the River Jordan, into the country I have promised will be yours. I never failed Moses and I will not fail you either, so be strong and brave-hearted! As long as you follow my laws, you will have nothing to fear. I will be with you always, and you will have victory!" Standing tall and steadfast, Joshua commanded his officers to prepare the people for the invasion without delay.

Excitement rippled through the camp as the news spread to get ready. After 40 years, the moment that the travelers had been waiting for had finally arrived! The Israelites were about to see for themselves the wonderful country that their grandparents, parents, brothers and sisters had struggled in vain to reach. And God had promised them success. The Promised Land would at last be theirs! Everyone was so eager that even though there were hundreds of thousands of people to mobilize, the preparations took only three days.

Meanwhile, Joshua sent two men on a dangerous secret mission. "Go and investigate the city of Jericho," he told them. "I want you to find out as much as you can about its defenses and its army." And the two spies slipped away.

Under cover, the men managed to dodge inside Jericho's gates and walk through the city, mingling with the enemy. After they had found out all they could, they went to the house of a woman named Rahab, who had promised to keep them safe for the night. But in the narrow streets of Jericho nothing went unseen. It didn't take long for neighborhood gossip and rumors to reach the ears of the king, who immediately sent soldiers to Rahab's house. "Open up by royal command!" they yelled, battering at the door. "Open up or we'll force the door down!"

Rahab remained perfectly calm. "Whatever are you making all this fuss about?" she smiled sweetly, welcoming the soldiers into her house.

"Where are they?" the soldiers snarled, upturning tables and dragging curtains aside . "Come on. We know you've got them—you're hiding two Israelites, foreign spies and enemies, in here somewhere!"

Rahab's faith
Rahab was a prostitute who lived in a house that formed part of the town wall of Jericho. She knew that the Israelites planned to capture the town, and she feared for her own life and for the lives of her family. Rahab had heard how God had helped the Israelites on their journey from Egypt, and she believed in His power. She declared her faith in God and begged the spies to save her family, in return for her helping them. When the Israelites destroyed Jericho, Rahab and her family were the only people who were spared.

Spies on a rope
The rope that Rahab used to help the spies escape could have been made of twisted hair or strips of animal skin. In Egypt, rope was also made from woven papyrus strips.

Spies
A spy is a person who secretly collects information on the activities, movements, and plans of an enemy and then reports this to someone else. Spying is often very dangerous work. This story illustrates the use of spies in Bible times, and they are still used all over the world today. Spies are also known as secret agents.

"Israelites? No!" Rahab gasped, pretending to be shocked. "You don't mean they were spies! It's true that two men came to stay with me, but I had no idea they were Israelites!" She paused, and then said, "In that case, I'm afraid you've missed them. They waited until darkness fell and then they went out somewhere." Rahab's voice grew urgent. "You'll have to hurry —it's nearly dark and the city gates are about to shut! They can't have gotten very far. If you go quickly, you might just catch them." The soldiers rushed out of the house in a terrible hurry and dashed off down the street.

The minute the soldiers were out of sight, Rahab rushed up to the roof, where she had hidden the Israelites under a heap of reeds that she had laid out to dry in the sun. The two men were highly relieved when they saw that the fingers uncovering them were Rahab's—not those belonging to the King of Jericho's soldiers!

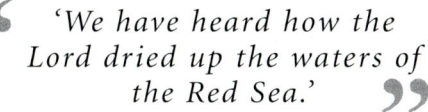
'We have heard how the Lord dried up the waters of the Red Sea.'

"It's too risky for you to stay here any longer," Rahab warned them in a whisper. "You must go and hide in the hills, where the soldiers can't find you. But before you go, please promise me one thing. Everyone here is terrified of your people. We know how the Red Sea parted and let you leave Egypt; we've heard how you crushed King Sihon and King Og and took their lands. Nearly everyone believes that God is on your side and that anyone who faces you is doomed. In return for the help I have given you, promise me

that you will spare me and my family when the Israelites come marching into Jericho."

The men took her hands. "When we attack, make sure everyone is locked inside your house and tie a scarlet cord at the window. We will then spare everyone inside, for the sake of the kindness you have shown us."

Rahab's house was built into the city wall itself. Opening up a window, she peered out nervously to see if anyone was around. Then she tied a rope firmly onto the ledge and flung the other end out into the darkness, listening to it tumble down a long way below. After a moment's anxious goodbye, the two Israelites climbed silently down, quite unseen, and escaped into the night.

Tribes of Canaan
When the Israelites arrived in the land of Canaan, there were already many tribes of people living there. The Bible tells us that the Canaanites were descended from Noah's son Ham and that the Israelites were descended from one of Noah's other sons, Shem. Noah said that the descendants of Shem would one day rule over Ham's descendants, which comes true at this point in the Bible. God tells the Israelites that they have to kill all the Canaanites, and that they are not allowed to live alongside them. This is because God knows that His people might be tempted to worship the gods of Canaan, like Baal. The tribes that the Israelites do not utterly defeat, such as the Midianites and the Philistines, appear as enemies of the Israelites later in the Bible. You can see here the spies escaping out of Rahab's window in the wall of Jericho.

GESHURITES
Haran
GREAT SEA
Megiddo
MIDIANITES
AMORITES
Shilon Mizpeh
AMMONITES
Jericho
JEBUSITES
Jebus
PHILISTINES
SALT SEA
Hebron
AVVITES
Beersheba
MOABITES
AMALEKITES
EDOMITES

❧ **ABOUT THE STORY** ❧
Joshua takes over Moses' role as God's servant. The Israelites are filled with excitement as the day of reaching the Promised Land draws near. However, all is nearly lost when soldiers begin searching for Joshua's spies. If Rahab had not hidden them, the invasion might have failed. The scarlet cord that Rahab ties outside her house to save her family is symbolic of the blood smeared outside doorways during Passover.

Crossing the Jordan

THE Israelites had faith in the Lord's promise that they would successfully storm Jericho, and when they heard the reports from Joshua's spies, they were elated. Now they knew that even their enemies believed that God was with them and shook with fear in anticipation of their coming. However, in order to attack the great city itself, the Israelites had to first find a way to cross the flood of the mighty River Jordan.

The morning came when Joshua gave the order to advance over the river bank, and the Israelites camped all over the plain, prepared to march. First to set off were the priests, who carried high the Ark of the Covenant for all to see. Following behind, a safe distance from the holiness of the ark, came 40,000 soldiers, armed and ready for war.

> **"** *The priests who bore the ark stood on dry ground in the midst of the Jordan.* **"**

❧ ABOUT THE STORY ❧

God tells Joshua that He is with him, just as He was with Moses before. And just as God held back the waters of the Red Sea, He now holds back the mighty Jordan so that the Israelites can cross the river and step onto the land God promised their ancestors so long ago. At last, their years of wandering in the desert are over. They build a memorial with 12 rocks from the riverbed, to mark the site of the amazing miracle.

Entering the Promised Land
After 40 long years in the wilderness, and many trials and lapses of faith, the Israelites entered the Promised Land. Led by Joshua, they made their way up the east side of the Salt Sea from the wilderness around Mount Sinai. They briefly made camp at Abel Shittim, before God led them into Canaan, and the Israelite nation witnessed the miraculous crossing of the River Jordan.

Altar by the Jordan
At Joshua's command the Israelites built an altar by the river. This was to remind the people of the miracle that God performed for them.

Closer and closer came the great crowd of people to the fast-flowing waters of the Jordan, with the city of Jericho looming ever larger on the opposite side. When the priests had reached the edge of the river, Joshua gave them God's command. "As soon as your feet are in the water, go no further." One by one the holy men stepped down into the Jordan, and as they stood still in the midst of the channel, with the ark raised aloft, they found that the water level began to lower. The Lord was holding back the river at a spot higher up the valley, preventing it from sweeping the Israelites away. As Joshua watched, the waters started to drain from around the priests' feet, and a dry path emerged across to the far bank. He wasted no time in giving the order for the army to advance, and rank by rank the troops marched past the sacred ark across the exposed riverbed.

When the very last soldier was safely on the opposite side of the Jordan, the Lord told Joshua to send a man from each Israelite tribe to fetch a rock from around the priests' feet. When this was done, the priests themselves moved off over the dried-up riverbed, step by step, carefully bringing the ark into the Promised Land. The moment the priests' feet reached the Jericho side, the Israelites heard a distant rumbling, like the sound of far-off thunder. The noise rapidly turned into a roar, then a deafening boom, and suddenly they saw the waters of the Jordan come crashing down the river bed once more, spraying over the channel and overflowing the banks, soaking the Israelites who were standing there, watching in awe as immense waves plunged onward, rushing down to the sea.

"Take these 12 rocks and build a memorial to mark the site of this miracle forever," Joshua commanded the stunned soldiers. Then the Israelites began to cheer.

The Israelites' trust in their new leader had been rewarded, and each soldier stood with awe and respect in his heart for Joshua, just as they had done for Moses. "We will follow you wherever you take us and do whatever you command," the people cried to Joshua. And they knew that God Himself was among them as they turned to face the army of the powerful city of Jericho.

A nation on the move
Some people have tried to figure out how many Israelites entered Canaan. The word *lp* is used in some Bible accounts, and people do not know what it means. Some think it means a thousand people and others "armed men." Depending on which meaning they use, the number varies between 500,000 and two million people.

THE PRIESTS CARRY THE ARK OF THE COVENANT INTO THE RIVER AHEAD OF THE PEOPLE. SINCE GOD'S HOME ON EARTH WAS BELIEVED TO BE BETWEEN THE WINGS OF THE ANGELS ON THE LID OF THE ARK, THIS WAS A SIGN TO THE PEOPLE THAT GOD WAS LEADING THEM TO THE PROMISED LAND.

The river runs dry
In 1927, an earthquake caused mud to block the River Jordan for 21 hours. God may have used natural forces to perform the miracle described in the story.

Fall of Jericho

JOSHUA and his 40,000 soldiers stood on the plain facing the great city of Jericho. Its towering stone walls stared blankly back at them—too high to climb, too thick to batter down—and the huge, sturdy city gates had been bolted and barred. Not even the smallest mouse would have found a chink in the defenses to creep in or out. There were no weak points for the Israelites to attack, and Joshua decided that there was nothing to do but sit and wait for the citizens to run out of food and water. But God had quite a different war plan and sent a messenger to tell Joshua what to do.

Following the Lord's commands, the next day the Israelite leader gave the soldiers the order to march. "Put on your armor and pick up your weapons," Joshua told them. "I want you to parade right around the outside of the city once, in full view of the enemy. The priests will go with you at the center of the march, carrying trumpets and holding high the Ark of the Covenant. Everyone is to be very careful not to utter a single word until I give the signal. I won't give the signal today, but you must all be ready for when I do. Then I want you to shout until your lungs are fit to burst." The soldiers were more than a little puzzled by this strange battle strategy, but they all had faith in their commander, so they set off around the city.

W HEN THE ISRAELITES HAD KILLED EVERYONE, THEY DESTROYED THE CITY. THE FIRST FRUITS OF THEIR CONQUEST OF CANAAN—THE CITY, WITH EVERYONE AND EVERYTHING IN IT— WERE OFFERED TO GOD ☙

Ancient Jericho
The place generally identified with Old Testament Jericho is the site of Tell es-Sultan (shown to the left). The first settlements grew up around an oasis. From about 8000 B.C. town after town was built and destroyed on the same site each time. Jericho is the oldest walled city in the world.

Trumpet call
The trumpets used by the priests in the story were called *shoars*. They were made of rams' horns, and were used to call people to battle and also to worship. The shoar is still used by rabbis today in some Jewish religious ceremonies.

The terrified inhabitants of Jericho watched and waited, listening to the fanfare of trumpets outside their walls. The full might of the Israelite army was on display, and the icy silence of the warriors made their blood run cold. The sight of the ark filled them with dread. They knew it was the sacred chest of the all-powerful Israelite God—the God who had helped them defeat the Egyptians and the Amorites. When would the attack come on their own city?

Every morning for six days the Israelites tramped their way around the city. Each time the people of Jericho saw the army, they prepared themselves to face an invasion; and each time the Israelites withdrew, they grew more and more anxious. Whatever were the Israelites up to?

When dawn broke on the seventh day, Joshua gave the army a new command: today they were to circle the city seven times. Imagine the panic that rose among the inhabitants of Jericho when they realized something was at last about to happen. The soldiers must have been able to hear the people's frightened cries. "Why aren't they stopping? They're not going back to their camp! Any minute now, they'll turn and head straight for us . . . . The ark will strike us down! The Israelites are coming!"

But the expected attack still didn't arrive. As soon as the ark had passed around the city seven times, Joshua gave the sign. The 40,000 soldiers opened their mouths and bellowed with all their strength, adding their voices to the blasts of the priests' trumpets.

The din was earsplitting. Inside Jericho, no one could hear themselves speak. The unearthly noise circled the entire city like the howling of souls in torment, pressing in on all sides and seeming to grow louder at every second.

> " *The people raised a great shout and the wall fell down flat.* "

Outside the city, the almighty noise echoed and re-echoed around the hills, and the Israelites felt the very ground beneath their feet begin to vibrate.

As the air throbbed, the earth trembled and then quaked, until with one great shudder the massive walls of Jericho came tumbling down. Immediately the soldiers rushed on the city, scrambling their way in over the heaps of crumbled stone. Only Rahab and her family were spared, just as the spies had promised. The fame of another Israelite victory spread far and wide across Canaan, and Joshua's name was spoken with fear throughout the land.

Fighting with bronze

Joshua's invasion of Jericho took place in about 1400 B.C. during a period known as the Late Bronze Age. Most weapons at this time were made of bronze. These pictures show some of the weapons the Israelites might have been carrying when they stormed into the city. They include battleaxes, a spearhead, a dagger and an arrowhead.

❧ ABOUT THE STORY ❧

This story shows that God is with the Israelites. He tells Joshua about the unusual way in which he must take the city of Jericho. Jericho is the first Canaanite city to be taken, and the Israelites honor God by devoting it to Him. The only citizens to be spared are Rahab and her family. She helped the Israelite spies, and this is God's recognition of that faithful act. After the defeat of Jericho, Joshua's fame spreads.

Battle of Ai

SPURRED on by the victory at Jericho, Joshua immediately sent scouts farther into the land of Canaan to check out their next target, the city of Ai. The news they brought back was encouraging. They felt that an army of two or three thousand soldiers should be able to defeat the city. But the ease with which Jericho had fallen had made the scouts overconfident. They had severely underestimated how fiercely the small population of Ai would fight to protect their city. The determined citizens forced back the warriors sent by Joshua, leaving many Israelites dead and chasing the rest away into the desert.

Joshua was deeply shocked. "Why, Lord?" the Israelite commander cried, striding up and down his tent. "Why have you let this happen?"

"What did you expect?" came the Lord's thunderous reply. "Israel has sinned against me!"

Joshua was baffled. "How? What do you mean?"

"There is one among you who has disobeyed my commands," roared the Lord. "Until he is found and punished, the Israelite nation must stand on its own!"

The next morning, Joshua gathered all the Israelites before him. Guided by God, his eyes slowly scanned the massive crowd, and came to rest on the tribe of Judah. In a steely voice, Joshua called for the households of the tribe to pass in front of him. As soon as Joshua saw the Zerahites, something made him shout, "Stop!" As the family stood trembling, Joshua slowly lifted an accusing finger. "You!" he breathed, pointing at a man called Achan. "You're the sinner who has brought God's wrath upon us!"

Achan immediately fell on his knees in front of the enraged Israelite leader and confessed. At the conquest of Jericho, Joshua had given strict orders that all precious booty was the property of the Lord, to be placed in the treasury for safekeeping. Yet Achan had stolen a beautiful mantle, along with some gold and silver, and hidden them.

Digging for history
Most of the discoveries that have been made about this time have come from archaeologists, people who learn about the past by digging up old buildings and objects. The archaeologists in the picture have found a place where they think ancient people lived—an archaeological site—and they are trying to find objects that have been left behind. For example, finding cooking pots may tell them what people ate at the time. There are specialists who study only the area around the Salt Sea, now called the Dead Sea, trying to find out about the people and places mentioned in the Bible. A lot of objects, like things made of leather or wood, did not survive, but enough has been found to give us a good idea of what life may have been like.

Luxury robe
This picture shows the type of robe that Achan might have stolen from Jericho. It would have been worn by a nobleman, and would have been made of expensive fabrics, richly embroidered and decorated.

The Lord told Joshua to try a second attack on the city of Ai and instructed him to set a clever trap. At night, 30,000 soldiers crept into the hills behind the city. Next day, while these troops lay in wait out of sight, the rest of the Israelite army attacked the city from the front. However, the soldiers of Ai were well prepared, and their king was delighted to find that, just as before, his fighters soon got the upper hand. Bit by bit, the Israelites were beaten back. Even when the order came for the Israelite army to retreat, the warriors of Ai didn't give up. They chased the retreating Israelites into the wilderness.

But, unbeknown to the King of Ai, everything had happened exactly according to plan. The Israelites had only pretended to be overcome in order to lure the fighters away from the city. Now the Israelite ambush rushed into Ai and began the destruction of the city.

> ❝ *Joshua burned Ai and made it forever a heap of ruins.* ❞

Out in the countryside, Joshua saw smoke start to rise as Ai was set on fire, and he gave the signal for his fleeing troops to turn and face their pursuers. With utter horror, the King of Ai realized they had been trapped. The invaders were closing in on his army from the front and from the city at the rear, and there was no hope of escape.

By sunset, the King of Ai's dead body hung from a tree. His army lay slain in the wilderness, and his people lay dead in the streets. All the kings of the lands beyond the Jordan swore to join forces to take revenge on the Israelites.

While the miserable man begged for mercy at Joshua's feet, messengers were sent to search his tent. They quickly returned with the stolen treasures. "God punished us for your wrongdoing by taking the lives of our soldiers," Joshua coldly told Achan. "Now, you must be punished, and pay the same price that they did." And then the people stoned Achan to death.

Shekels
The Bible tells us that Achan stole "two hundred shekels of silver, and a wedge of gold of 50 shekels' weight." The shekel was not a coin, but a weight. Most of the people at this time measured amounts of silver and gold in terms of how much they weighed, rather than how much they were worth.

Achan's death
This picture shows Achan being punished for his sin. In the Bible, we are told that after the stoning, Achan was burned, together with his oxen, his sheep and goats, his tent and all that he had. He had committed a sin against God, which all the Israelites had suffered for, so according to the law God gave to Moses on Mount Sinai he had to be punished.

⊹ **ABOUT THE STORY** ⊹

God brings about the Israelites' defeat at Ai because He knows Achan has disobeyed Him. He punishes all the people for one man's sin. This can be compared to the way in which Adam's sin affected the whole of humanity. Once Achan has been punished, the Israelites have God's blessing again, and their second attack is a success. This story shows that God will always find those who disobey Him and will punish them.

Tricked by the Gibeonites

NOT far to the southwest of Ai lay the mighty city of Gibeon. The Gibeonites were a strong and powerful people, but news of how Joshua had razed the great city of Jericho to the ground and slaughtered the people of Ai had struck fear into their hearts. The Israelites weren't far away, and the Gibeonites knew that if they waited for the Israelites to arrive they might suffer the same fate as the people who were once their neighbors. Instead, the Gibeonites made a clever plan . . . .

Joshua was resting in his tent where the Israelites had camped at Gilgal when a messenger suddenly dashed in. "The scouts have reported that strangers are approaching, sir," he panted, all out of breath.

Joshua sat up, immediately alert and ready for action. "Send soldiers out to meet them and escort them to me," he commanded. He was always suspicious when anyone was seen heading for their huge army camp.

When the strangers were brought to his tent, Joshua was amazed. These weren't royal messengers sent from any Canaanite king, they were just a ragged group of peasants! Joshua found himself facing a dirty, stinking group of exhausted people, whose patched clothes were in tatters and whose worn-out shoes were falling off their feet. "At last we have found you!" they cried, falling on their knees

with gratitude in front of Joshua. "We have been traveling for many weeks to get here. Even though we live far away, news of your wonderful God has reached our tribe. You are obviously a blessed people, and we would like to join you. Our elders have sent us as ambassadors to ask you to make a treaty with us."

Joshua was not convinced by the flattery. "How can I be sure that you are who you say you are?" he queried. "The tribes of Canaan know well that we have sworn never to make peace with them. You might therefore be people from the very cities we plan to attack, come in disguise to try to trick us into making peace."

Wine
There are frequent references to both drinking and making wine in the Bible, for the land was well suited to growing vines.

Baking bread
The Gibeonites in the story carry bread in their packs. Bread was the most important food in this area at the time. The picture shows an Egyptian model of two servants baking bread. One is sitting down and tending the fire, while the other servant is kneading the dough. The model dates from around 1900 B.C.

It took the Israelite army only three days to reach the city of Gibeon, and Joshua realized his dreadful blunder at once. His first guess had been completely right—the travelers were local people who had dressed up to trick him, to try to escape death at the hands of a huge army led by God Himself. Joshua was furious that he'd allowed himself to be persuaded by their story, but it was now too late. Even though the soldiers were eager to attack and take their revenge, Joshua knew that to break his solemn vow to let them live would bring God's wrath upon them, even though they would have killed them all had they not made the peace. The Gibeonites were therefore spared, but as punishment for their lies they were taken as slaves to spend the rest of their days working for the great Israelite army and the tabernacle of their God.

> 66 *'Now you are cursed, and you shall always be slaves for the house of my God.'* 99

The dejected travelers reached inside their packs and produced hunks of stale, moldy bread and battered, torn wineskins. "When we set off from our homes, this bread was still warm from the oven and the wineskins were brand new," they said, earnestly. "Please make our long, hard journey worthwhile. We beg you to make a peace treaty with our people."

Joshua granted the travelers their precious peace treaty, and all the Israelite elders swore to let their people live. The tattered group were eager to be off with their wonderful news, and they hurried away from the Israelite camp at once. After all, they had many weeks of traveling ahead before they would reach home . . . .

Carved in stone
This Egyptian stone contains the first mention of the nation of Israel outside the Bible. It dates from around 1230 B.C. when Pharaoh Mereneptah was ruling. The inscription on the stone describes his military campaign in Canaan and says that he defeated the Israelites.

Canaanite man
The picture on this Egyptian glazed brick shows what a nobleman from Canaan might have looked like at around the time the Israelites settled in the area.

⊷ **ABOUT THE STORY** ⊷

Joshua makes a treaty of peace with the Gibeonites, and the Israelites swear a solemn oath not to harm them. Oaths were regularly used in treaties, as a way of enforcing the terms. Once Joshua realizes that he has been tricked, it is too late. He has to honor the treaty.

The Longest Day

KING Adonizedek of Jerusalem was among the Canaanite rulers who had sworn to join forces to drive the Israelites out of Canaan. He knew that presenting a strong, united front was their only hope against the massive Israelite army. The fall of the mighty city of Jericho had spelled out disaster for any city that tried to stand alone. Now the Gibeonites had weakened their number by betraying the Amorite kings' pact. In saving themselves from destruction, they had abandoned everyone else to a more certain doom, and Adonizedek was enraged. He immediately sent messengers to the four kings that neighbored his lands, saying, "The Gibeonites have made peace with the enemy. I say we should destroy the city of

> **The sun stood still and the moon stayed, until the nation took vengeance.**

Gibeon ourselves. Send your armies right away, and together we'll take our revenge on these deserters." So King Hoham of Hebron, King Piram of Jarmuth, King Japhia of Lachish, and King Debir of Eglon immediately mobilized their forces and declared war on their onetime ally.

Gibeon was soon under siege. The citizens had scarcely finished celebrating how they had tricked the fearsome Israelites, when the five savage armies of the hill kings surrounded them on all sides, and the city found itself in the very position it had tried so hard to avoid! The

Defeated enemies
On the left is a decorative plaque showing the first king of Egypt, King Narmer, holding a defeated enemy by the hair. On the right is a picture of an Israelite with his foot on the neck of an enemy. Both these images show typical gestures of subjection of enemies after battle. It was a sign that the enemy knew they had been defeated. In the Bible, we are told that Joshua's captains put their feet on the necks of the five defeated kings. As Joshua marched through Canaan, his army defeated many more cities along the way. These cities were called city-states.

Gibeonite leaders now sent messengers to their former enemy to beg for help to get them out of trouble.

The news that the Amorite kings of the hills had gathered against Gibeon reached Joshua in the middle of the night, but he immediately gave the army the order to march. There would be no better chance to crush several important Canaanite tribes at once, and God reassured Joshua of victory. Without waiting for daybreak Joshua made the army strike camp immediately, marching all night through the darkness.

The Israelite attack came as a complete surprise. While all the Amorite forces were facing Gibeon, half-asleep and half-awake, the full strength of the Israelite army fell on them from behind. The soldiers panicked. Some stayed to fight and were hacked down as the Israelites rushed upon them. Others turned and tried to flee. But even though they were out of reach of the Israelite swords, suddenly the Lord sent huge hailstones the size of rocks from above, stoning them to death as they ran.

Then Joshua gave a mighty shout. "Sun, stand still in the sky! Moon, hang where you are in the heavens! Let time itself be stopped until we have crushed these enemies completely!" To the horror of the Amorite armies, the Lord heard Joshua's plea. Hour after hour, the Israelites continued to hack down their enemies, yet the day didn't get any shorter.

In the midst of the killing, a messenger came running up to Joshua excitedly. "Sir, the five kings tried to escape, but some of our troops found them," he told Joshua. "They were hiding in a cave at Makkedah, but we've now got them cornered. What shall we do with them?"

Joshua wanted to deal with the rebel kings himself, to make an example of them to any other Canaanite peoples that might dare go against the Israelites. "Block the cave mouth up with rocks," he instructed the messenger. "That will hold them fast until we've finished destroying everything they own!" And while the Amorite kings were locked up, the Israelites slaughtered their people.

At the end of the extraordinarily long day, the Israelites had crushed five of their strongest enemies. When not one Amorite soldier remained alive, Joshua gave the command for the five kings to be brought out of the cave. He threw them to the ground in front of the Israelite war leaders. "You should never be afraid, people of Israel!" Joshua cried. "For this is what the Lord has promised will happen to our enemies." In front of the Israelites, the kings were hanged, one by one, and their bodies thrown back into the cave from which they had just come.

❧ ABOUT THE STORY ❧

God reassures Joshua that He is with him and that the Israelites will win. When the battle begins, God sends hailstones, which rain down on the enemy from above. Then He grants Joshua's request and makes the sun stand still. The day does not end until the Israelites have defeated their enemies. In the Bible, we are told that there was no day like that before or after it. This is another great success for Joshua.

Light or darkness?
The Longest Day in this story is usually interpreted to mean that daylight lasted longer than usual. However, it could be that the story refers to an eclipse of the sun, which would mean that the darkness of the night lasted longer than usual. There is no mention of it being daylight, so it could be that the darkness helped the Israelites win.

Dividing the Promised Land

NOT content with having slain the five Amorite kings and crushing their armies, Joshua next attacked and destroyed each of their cities, killing every person found there. News of the terrible bloodshed spread immediately through Canaan, and, with hearts full of dread, the Canaanite chiefs realized that no one stood a chance of being spared. Their choice was either to sit back and wait for their people to be slaughtered, or to come out and fight. So, under the leadership of King Jabin of Hazor, the rulers mobilized their armies. Hundreds of thousands of troops, horses, and chariots gathered in a massive camp at Merom. The soldiers were all in full battle dress and they were all very determined to stop the Israelites from taking their homeland.

Report after report reached Joshua's ears of the vast army preparing to attack. But God reassured him. "Have no fear," He told Joshua, "for I will deliver all these troops slain into your hands. Tomorrow, you will kill their horses and burn their chariots." Joshua trusted the Lord and immediately led the Israelites into an attack. The battle was more savage and bloody than any either army had suffered before. When the ruthless killing was eventually over, the bodies littering the battlefield were Canaanite. As God had vowed, they lay next to the corpses of their horses and the smoking wrecks of their once-glorious chariots. The Israelites had won their mightiest victory yet.

For several more years, Joshua was to continue waging wars against the Canaanite tribes, conquering more and more of the Promised Land until at last most of the country was theirs. Then the fighting ceased. It was time to divide up the land among the 12 Israelite tribes.

The boldest Israelite elders made haste to lay claim to

the areas they wanted for their families or that they thought were rightfully theirs. One of the first to get his allocation was Caleb, Moses' courageous scout and now an old man of 85, who finally received the reward the Lord had promised him. For having faith in God's order to invade Canaan when everyone else was fainthearted, Joshua granted him the great city of Hebron and the surrounding hill country. However, not everyone was as sure about which part of the beautiful country they wanted to live in. Seven tribes simply couldn't decide! So after sending three men from each to survey the land, Joshua divided it up into seven parts, and the tribe chiefs drew lots for their new homes.

The only tribe not to be given an entire area was the Levites, whom God had long ago chosen to be His priests. They were given 48 cities in different parts of the country, so they could lead the Israelites in worship. The tabernacle itself was set up permanently in the city of Shiloh, at the heart of the Promised Land.

Finally the Lord told Joshua to appoint six cities as Cities of Refuge. In these places, people accused of crimes would be protected against those wanting to take their revenge, and they would be assured a fair trial.

With the country organized, the Israelites began to move into their allocated areas. But it wasn't always easy. Handfuls of Canaanite people still stubbornly remained in some far-flung places, and the powerful Israelite families had to either drive them off their land or force them into slavery. The Reubenites and Gadites fell into particular trouble. Along with half the tribe of Manasseh, they were given, by Joshua, some of the first lands the Israelites had conquered— the plains of Moab. However, these lay on the far side of the Jordan. These tribes were concerned that the river acted as a boundary dividing them from the rest of the Israelites.

delivered us from slavery in Egypt and worked miracles for us and gave us the Promised Land! We will serve the Lord truly! He is our only God!"

With trembling hands, the elderly war chief motioned for the huge throng of Israelites to be calm. "If you do wrong and turn to sin, you will not be forgiven," he warned the waiting crowd. "If you forsake the Lord and turn to worshiping idols and false gods, you will bring the full force of His wrath down upon you."

Undeterred, the Israelites replied as if with one voice, "We will serve the Lord our God! We will obey Him and do whatever He tells us."

Joshua was content that the people were speaking from their hearts and that they really meant what they were promising. Finally, he felt that he could die in peace. Taking the holy book of God's laws, he wrote in it that the Israelites had renewed their covenant. Then, slowly but steadily, the great leader took a large stone from nearby and set it up in the sanctuary of the Lord. "This rock has heard everything that has passed between us and God today," he told the committed people. "If you disobey the Lord, it will bear witness that you have broken your word, and you will be punished for your sins."

Not long afterward, the battle-scarred warrior passed away. Amid great grief and mourning, the Israelites carried his body to the part of the Promised Land where he had made his home, the high hill country of Ephraim, and there they laid him to rest.

The battle still to be fought

Joshua was a great warrior and a mighty leader, but when he died he had not conquered all Israel. This map shows the cities he had not conquered. The Philistines were particularly difficult to defeat, and their fortified towns, such as Gaza and Gath, remained undefeated until the reign of King David. This meant that all around the Israelites there were people worshiping idolatrous gods, like Baal and Ashtoreth, and this proved to be too much of a temptation after Joshua's death.

Ancient city

One of the cities captured by Joshua in his long battle to gain complete control of the Promised Land was called Megiddo. King Solomon later chose Megiddo as one of his main fortified cities outside Jerusalem. The site where ancient Megiddo stood is believed to be Tell el-Mutesellim, in northwest Israel. Archaeologists who have dug there have found evidence of a large town that, at different times, contained stables, storehouses, palaces, office-type buildings and a gateway.

❖ ABOUT THE STORY ❖

Joshua is soon to die, and no single person will take over his role as leader. He reminds the Israelites of their history and how God has helped them at every step, from their escape from Egypt to their new lives in Israel. The Israelites choose to renew their covenant with God.

Israelites Disobey the Judges

FOR a long time after Joshua's death, the Israelites were careful to keep their promise to obey God's commands and live according to His laws. Without a war chief or king at the nation's head, it was up to the wise officials called Judges to bind the people together in their single faith. However, as the years went by, the brave men and women who had invaded Canaan grew old and passed away. There were no longer eyewitnesses to tell of all the wonderful things that God had done for the Israelites, so many people began to wonder whether they had ever happened at all. Perhaps the miracles of crossing the River Jordan dry-footed, and the miraculous collapse

of the walls of Jericho, and the day that the sun stood still for Joshua and his warriors, were just the stuff of legends.

One of Joshua's last orders had been to drive out all the inhabitants of Canaan. Even though the Israelite war parties continued to have great success in taking new territories, they sometimes allowed the local people to remain as slaves. Other times, the Israelites simply moved into areas and settled down among the tribes. The Judges often repeated Joshua's warning about what would happen if the Israelites mixed with the Canaanites: the temptation to follow the pagan gods would prove too much, and the Lord would turn away from them in anger, resulting in the fall of the nation. And the time indeed came when an angel came down from heaven with a final caution that God was losing patience. "It's thanks only to the Lord that you were brought safely out of Egypt and into the land He swore to give your ancestors," the angel said, sternly. "He made a special covenant with the Israelite nation; your part of the bargain was to drive out the pagan people from this land and break down their altars to false gods. Now God finds you have disobeyed His commands and are living among these unbelievers. The Lord will no longer fight these tribes for you, and if you aren't careful, your neighbors will become your enemies."

At this threat the despairing Israelites wept with remorse and prayed for forgiveness. But it wasn't long before they were carrying on just as before. God's anger grew as His chosen people turned their backs on Him, and in His turn He withdrew His protection.

Without God on their side, the Israelites soon found themselves in the hands of King Eglon of Moab. The

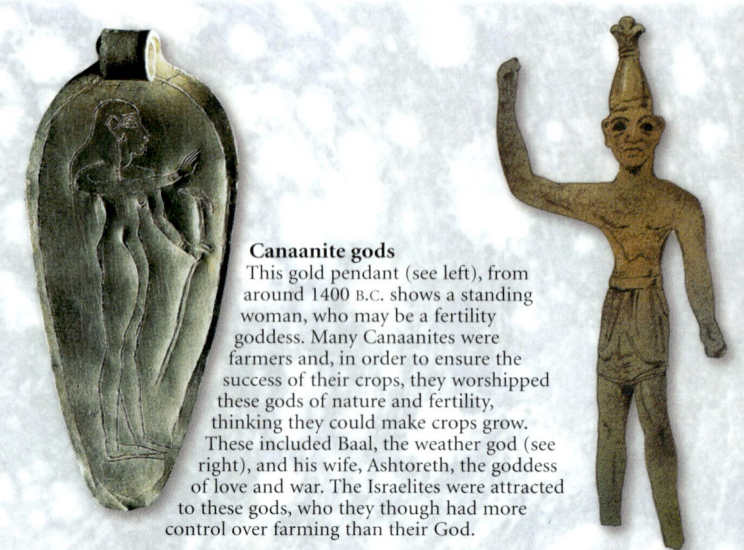

❧ ABOUT THE STORY ❧

Despite the angel's warning, the Israelites begin to forget God's laws. They live alongside the Canaanites, and start to worship their gods. The judges try to enforce God's laws but in vain. Finally, God loses patience and removes His protection. The Israelites fall under the control of their neighbors. It is only because of the bravery of Ehud that the Israelites win back God's favor, and their freedom.

Canaanite gods
This gold pendant (see left), from around 1400 B.C. shows a standing woman, who may be a fertility goddess. Many Canaanites were farmers and, in order to ensure the success of their crops, they worshipped these gods of nature and fertility, thinking they could make crops grow. These included Baal, the weather god (see right), and his wife, Ashtoreth, the goddess of love and war. The Israelites were attracted to these gods, who they though had more control over farming than their God.

his roof chamber. No sooner had Eglon closed the doors behind them than Ehud drew a two-edged sword and stabbed it into the king's stomach. In horror, as he lay dying, Eglon realized that Ehud was left-handed, and his soldiers must have checked for weapons only on the usual side of the body.

By the time King Eglon's servants had realized something was wrong, Ehud had escaped from the palace and was nearly home. The minute he reached Ephraim, he took out a trumpet and gave the signal to go to battle. The Israelites swooped down on the Moabite soldiers and slaughtered 10,000 of them. Finally, they had won back the Lord's favor and their freedom.

> *The people of Israel did what was evil in the sight of the Lord.*

Israelites lived under Moabite control for 18 long years—plenty of time for them to think back on the ways they had offended God and to feel true repentance. Yet at last God chose to give His betrayers yet another chance and answered their cries for help.

A party of Israelites had gone one day to pay tribute at the Moabite court, and King Eglon had received their gifts and sent them on their way when he suddenly received word that one of them had returned—a man named Ehud— saying he had a secret message. Intrigued, Eglon agreed to give him another audience. However, Ehud insisted that his message was private and for the king's ears alone. Still more curious, Eglon hurried Ehud up to

❈ THE JUDGES OF ISRAEL ❈

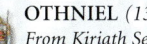

OTHNIEL *(1374–1334 B.C.)*
From Kiriath Sepher in Judah.
Saved the Israelites from the armies of western Mesopotamia.

EHUD *(1316–1236 B.C.)*
From Benjamin.
Saved the Israelites from the Moabites, the Ammonites, and the Amalekites.

SHAMGAR
Was a judge during the early rule of Deborah. Killed six hundred Philistines.

ABIMELECH
Ruled for three years. From Manasseh.

TOLA *(1126–1103 B.C.)*
A minor judge.
From Issachar.

JAIR *(1103–1081 B.C.)*
A wealthy man and a minor judge.
From Gilead, in east Manasseh.

IBZAN *(1100–1093 B.C.)*
A minor judge.
From Bethlehem, in Judah.

ELON *(1093–1083 B.C.)*
A minor judge.
From Zebulun.

ABDON *(1083–1077 B.C.)*
From Ephraim. A minor judge.

SAMSON *(1103–1083 B.C.)*
From Dan.
Attacked the Philistines.
Was betrayed by Delilah.

ELI *(ruled for 40 years)*
Was the priest at the tabernacle at Shiloh. Became Samuel's guardian.

SAMUEL *(1059–1043 B.C.)*
The last judge and a prophet. Brought the nation of Israel together. Under him, the Philistine invasions ended.

Deborah the Judge

THE Israelite people knew that from the very earliest times in their history, each time they had turned away from God and broken His commands, they had brought a severe punishment upon themselves. Surely the years that the Lord had allowed the ruthless Moabites to rule over them—the worst sentence yet—should have taught them a lesson they wouldn't forget? Unfortunately, this wasn't so. When Ehud died, the people quickly fell back into their old habits. Yet again the furious Lord turned his back on His people, leaving them to their own fate, and yet again they were conquered by an enemy: this time King Jabin of the Philistines. Now Jabin's army was feared far and wide—not only because it was under the command of the famous General Sisera, but also for its squadron of 900 indestructible iron chariots. The threat of his crack troops hovered over the Israelites, and King Jabin ruled the nation harshly for 20 years.

At that time, there was a prophetess named Deborah, who lived in the hill country of Ephraim. Deborah had been appointed one of Israel's judges, and she was well respected by the people for her wise counsel and just decisions. Totally unexpectedly, a man named Barak received a message that Deborah wanted to see him, and although he was very puzzled, he went at once to meet her. "The Lord commands you to gather 10,000 men and go to Mount Tabor," Deborah told him. "There, God will bring General Sisera and King Jabin's army out to fight you, and you will win!" Barak was more than a little startled; he was totally amazed! However, he agreed to do

as he was told—just as long as Deborah went too. "Of course I will go with you," she assured him. "But, even though you will be victorious in the battle, the greatest glory will not be yours. Sisera himself will be defeated by a woman." Undeterred, Barak steeled himself to his task and set about finding soldiers.

The news reached General Sisera that the Israelites were gathering on the slopes of Mount Tabor, intent on rebelling, and he at once prepared his forces for war. How frightened the Israelites must have been, facing line after line of chariots and row after row of accomplished,

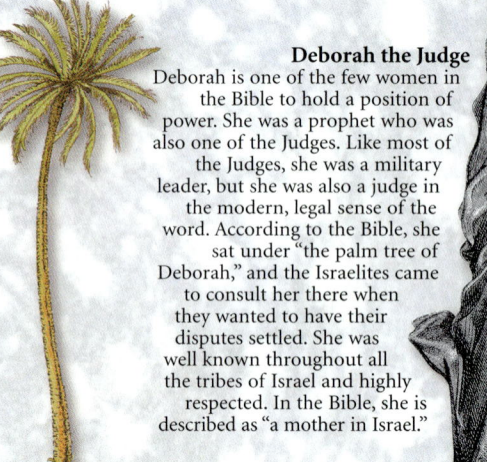

❧ ABOUT THE STORY ❧

Once again, the Israelites have forgotten God and are worshiping the gods of the Canaanites. So, once again, God removes His protection, and the Israelites come under the rule of King Jabin. After 20 years of hardship, Deborah comes to the rescue of her people, instructing Barak to gather an army. Deborah joins him, and together they defeat Jabin's army. Jael deceives General Sisera and kills him.

Deborah the Judge
Deborah is one of the few women in the Bible to hold a position of power. She was a prophet who was also one of the Judges. Like most of the Judges, she was a military leader, but she was also a judge in the modern, legal sense of the word. According to the Bible, she sat under "the palm tree of Deborah," and the Israelites came to consult her there when they wanted to have their disputes settled. She was well known throughout all the tribes of Israel and highly respected. In the Bible, she is described as "a mother in Israel."

professionally trained soldiers! But Deborah urged them on and inspired them with faith. "Up and fight, Israel!" she cried, before they went into attack. "Today, the Lord will deliver this great army into your hands."

Deborah's words proved true, and, against all the odds, Sisera's army was utterly routed. But when the fighting was finished and there was not a single Canaanite warrior left alive, the most important corpse of all was not to be found on the battlefield. Sisera had escaped.

Stumbling through the hills in a panic, the general was completely shocked by the defeat and physically drained. Yet somehow he managed to dodge all the Israelite troops combing the area, trying to hunt him down. In a clever move, he made for the tent of a woman named Jael—an unlikely hiding place as Jael was originally Israelite. However, her husband—a direct descendant from Moses' father-in-law—had changed his loyalties, having split from his tribe and made peace with King Jabin. As Sisera had hoped, Jael readily smuggled him inside her tent—which was just as well, since he was utterly exhausted and could go no farther. Kindly, Jael covered the slumped army chief with a rug, assuring him that he could sleep safely while she kept watch. Little did the general know that he was never to wake up. While Sisera dreamed, Jael hammered a tent peg right through his skull.

Even though Jabin's army was gone and his warlord dead, Barak and the Israelites didn't rest. The warriors carried on fighting until they had slain the Canaanite king himself and destroyed his palace at Hazor. Now surely this time the Israelites would make sure they did everything as the Lord wanted. Alas, no. Within the space of 40 years the

obstinate people had again turned to wicked ways, and an enraged God left them to be conquered by the Midianites.

> " *The Lord will sell Sisera into the hands of a woman.* "

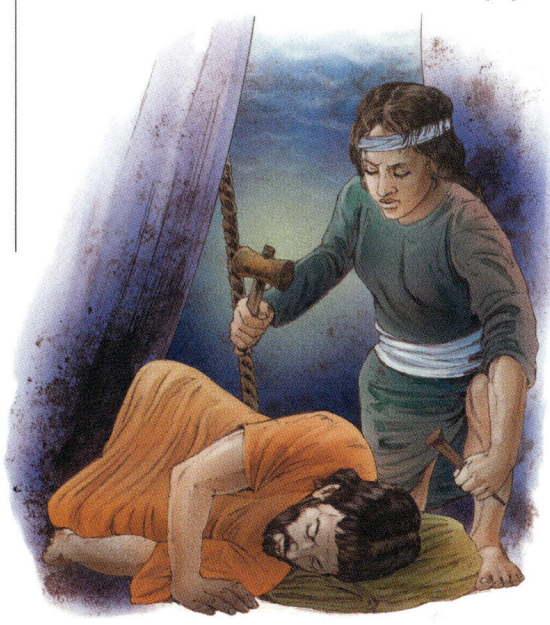

THE SONG OF DEBORAH

MOST BLESSED OF WOMEN BE JAEL,
THE WIFE OF HEBER THE KENITE,
OF TENT-DWELLING WOMEN MOST BLESSED.
HE ASKED WATER AND SHE GAVE HIM MILK,
SHE BROUGHT HIM CURDS IN A LORDLY BOWL.
SHE PUT HER HAND TO THE TENT PEG
AND HER RIGHT HAND TO THE
WORKMAN'S MALLET;
SHE STRUCK SISERA A BLOW,
AT HER FEET HE SANK, HE FELL;
WHERE HE SANK, THERE HE FELL DEAD.

The Song of Deborah
The Song of Deborah is one of the earliest passages in the Old Testament. It is a victory song—a celebration of the Israelites' victory over General Sisera. The song explains the details of the battle and Sisera's defeat.

Flooding of the river
Part of *The Song of Deborah* tells exactly how the Israelites won the battle. God sent a storm, which caused the River Kishon to flood. Sisera's chariots, which were in this area, were swept away. The Israelite soldiers were unharmed, as they were positioned on higher ground, on Mount Tabor.

Gideon and the Angel

THE Midianite tribes hated the Israelites with a passion and treated them more cruelly than any previous enemy. They made life as miserable for the Israelites as possible: they attacked their homes whenever they had the chance; and they burned their crops and killed their flocks, leaving the land wasted and the Israelites starving.

In these difficult times, the Israelites were forced to go to great lengths to try to outwit the Midianites, such as threshing any small amounts of wheat they could save in the wine press to keep it out of sight. A young farmer named Gideon was doing just this one day when a man appeared beside him out of nowhere. "You have a brave heart," the man told Gideon. "God is with you."

Gideon thought the man's words were even more odd than the weird way he had suddenly arrived. "If the Lord is indeed with us, how come we live under such terror?" he answered, bitterly. "Why doesn't God perform some amazing miracle to save us, like He did for our fathers? I tell you, the Lord has given up on us and left us to be punished by our enemies."

The stranger looked at Gideon without blinking. "You will take on the Midianites and set Israel free," he said.

"How on earth can I do that?" he scoffed. "My clan is the weakest, and I'm the youngest in my family!"

"The Lord will be with you," replied the stranger.

Still full of doubts, Gideon went off to find some food and drink to offer the uninvited guest. But when he laid down the meat and bread in front of him, the man only touched it with the tip of his staff. Instantly, the food burst into flames and the stranger disappeared. Gideon realized that he had been face to face with an angel.

Later that evening, a voice spoke to Gideon out of the darkness: it was the Lord Himself, instructing him to destroy his own father's altar to Baal and erect one to God instead. Gideon was afraid—he knew he'd be in very serious trouble. But that night, he did as he had been told. The people were furious when they saw what had been done and immediately suspected Gideon. Joash, Gideon's father, refused to punish his son, for he felt sure that there must be a good reason for his son's outburst.

From that day onward, Gideon was somehow different. But it was only when the Midianites, the Amalekites, and all the other Eastern tribes crossed the Jordan and gathered ready for a battle that Gideon showed exactly how much the Spirit of the Lord had altered him. Sounding a trumpet to call the Israelites to arms, he roused the people to strike back. A massive force

❧ ABOUT THE STORY ❧

Again, God rejects His people, and they fall into the hands of the Midianites, under whom they suffer great hardship. Then God chooses their savior, Gideon. Though afraid for his life, Gideon does as God asks and destroys his father's altar, building a new altar to God. Then he gathers an army and defeats the Midianites. Gideon refuses to rule over the Israelites, telling them that the Lord is their ruler.

Gideon and the angel
This picture shows Gideon talking to the angel. At first, Gideon is doubtful about the angel's message that he will save Israel. He does not think himself worthy. He asks for a sign from God, and when he sees the food burst into flames, he accepts God's will.

> ## With the 300 men that lapped I will give the Midianites into your hand.

of 32,000 men quickly formed—but the Lord told him the army was too big! "If this many Israelites defeat the Midianites, they'll think that they've done it," God told Gideon, "I want them to know that the victory is my work." Gideon gave permission for all those who were afraid to return home, and soon only 10,000 soldiers remained. "They are still too many," God said. "Take them down to the water and watch how they drink. If anyone laps the water like a dog, take him to one side. Tell those who scoop up the water with cupped hands that they're no longer needed." Before long, Gideon's army was down to a mere 300 men, and God was satisfied that with this number in their army, they would know whom to thank for their victory. So Gideon prepared his battle plan.

That night, three squads of 100 men crept from all directions up to the Midianite camp, each with a trumpet and a pitcher with a blazing torch inside. On Gideon's signal, the men blasted away and smashed their pitchers so that their torches flashed from all around in the darkness. In the confusion, the troops thought they were being attacked by a mighty army, and they ended up fighting among themselves. As panic spread, the troops began to flee, but they could not escape. Gideon sent messengers to Ephraim, where fighting men joined the chase.

The Israelites gave pursuit until the enemy were utterly defeated. The rejoicing nation begged Gideon to become their sole leader, but the young man refused. "I will not rule over you, and my son will not rule over you; the Lord will rule over you," he told the people. And Israel lived in peace for the rest of Gideon's life.

Asherah
In the Bible, God tells Gideon to destroy his father's altar to Baal, the Canaanite god, and to cut down the "asherah" beside it. Asherah is the name of a Canaanite fertility goddess associated with Baal, and an asherah pole is an image of that goddess, which would generally have been carved out of one big tree-trunk.

Pottery jars
The picture to the left shows the type of pottery pitcher, or jar, that Gideon and his men would have taken with them on the night that they attacked and defeated the Midianites.

Canaanite goddess
This limestone relief shows a Canaanite goddess standing under an arch of flowers. It was decorated with red paint, traces of which can still be seen. Unlike the Israelites, the Canaanites made images of their gods and goddesses and worshiped these.

Jephthah

IMMEDIATELY after Gideon died, Israel's troubles began once more. One of Gideon's sons, Abimelech, couldn't get over how his father had passed up the chance to be ruler of all Israel. He was tormented by thoughts of the missed opportunity, so he tricked his kinsmen out of a lot of money and paid thugs to kill all 70 of his brothers, before setting himself up as the King of Shechem and Bethmillo. But his supporters began to argue and fight among themselves, and after things in his country got worse, Abimelech was eventually killed when a woman dropped a millstone on his head.

> **"** *Jephthah crossed over to the Ammonites and he smote 20 cities.* **"**

Within 50 years the Israelites faced yet more chaos. The Ammonite people declared war on the Israelites. As the Israelites had done in the past, they cried out to the Lord for help. At first the Lord hardened His heart, but just in time He decided to give them another great war leader.

The man the Lord chose as His new hero might have been considered unsuitable in many ways. Jephthah was the son of a man named Gilead, but, since he had been born illegitimate, he was despised by all the members of Gilead's lawful family. As soon as his brothers had grown old enough to gang up against him, they had driven him away from home. Left to fend for himself in the land of Tob, Jephthah had made a name for himself as a fearsome bandit. Under his leadership, a band of villains had plundered the countryside, terrorizing the local people.

Jephthah's daughter
Human sacrifice was not something God would be pleased by, so this element of the story is surprising. It has been suggested that, instead of sacrificing his daughter, Jephthah sent her away to live a life of celibacy, in service to God. Other sources argue, however, that this is incompatible with the fact that the Bible clearly states that Jephthah kept his vow.

Timbrels and cymbals
Percussion instruments, such as cymbals and timbrels, or tambourines, were used to accompany singing and dancing. During the Exodus from Egypt, Moses' sister, Miriam, played a tambourine while she and the other women sang and danced. Israelite women would often celebrate the return of victorious armies by coming out of the town, singing and dancing with their timbrels.

Spoils of battle
This picture shows a gold amulet, or charm, in the shape of a flying falcon. It is now in the Israel Museum in Jerusalem. This is the type of valuable ornament that Jephthah and his men would have plundered from the towns they conquered.

Now the Israelites faced the full force of the Ammonite army, and a ruthless warrior such as Jephthah was just the kind of commander they needed to organize their counter-attack. The elders of the tribes hurried to the land of Tob to beg the man who had been disowned by his Israelite brothers to come back and lead their troops into battle. "I will return with you only on one condition," Jephthah demanded. "That if the Lord grants us victory, you will make me your leader." The panic-stricken Israelite elders quickly agreed to his demand.

Messengers soon arrived from the King of the Ammonites, demanding the return of land the Israelites had taken when they had originally invaded Canaan. Jephthah wasted no time in sending a clear message right back that they would not do so. "The Lord will judge this day between the people of Israel and the Ammonites!" he cried, rousing the soldiers to fight. Then Jephthah prayed to God and made a solemn vow, "Lord, if you deliver these enemies into our hands, I will sacrifice to you whatever I see first when I reach home." And so Jephthah and his army went to war and slaughtered the Ammonite forces.

News of the warlord's great victory traveled ahead of him, and as Jephthah drew near to his house his daughter came out to celebrate his return, playing a tambourine. Jephthah couldn't believe his eyes. Instead of rushing to throw his arms around his daughter, he howled with grief, throwing himself down into the dirt and tearing at his clothes in despair. "I have vowed to the Lord that I would sacrifice the first thing I saw on my return," he wept, unable to meet her eyes. "And I cannot take back my promise," he moaned. Jephthah's daughter bore the dreadful news with courage and faith. "It is right that you keep your bargain with God," she said quietly. "Only grant me some time to prepare myself."

After two months had passed, Jephthah paid the price for the wicked things he had done in the past, slaying his daughter by his own hand. But each year afterward, on the anniversary of her death, the Israelite women gathered together to remember her.

The journeys of Jephthah

When Jephthah was rejected by his family, he fled north from his home to the land of Tob. Here he made a name for himself as a great leader and a fearsome bandit. When Israel was being threatened by the Ammonites, the elders of the threatened tribes thought that Jephthah was the person to help them out. So they went to see him to ask if he would rescue them. Jephthah led his armies throughout the area to the east of the Jordan, destroying and burning the Ammonite towns, such as Abel-keramim, and defeating the Ammonites at every stage. With God on his side, the Ammonites could not win. But his foolish attempt to make a deal with God proves his undoing, when on his return to Mizpah his daughter is the first person to come out of his house to meet him, so he has to sacrifice her as he has vowed.

❧ ABOUT THE STORY ❧

After more years of trouble, God chooses a new leader, Jephthah. When the Israelites ask him to lead their troops into battle against the Ammonites, he makes a bargain with them that he remain their leader if he is successful. However, his bargain with God is not so clever. Unfortunately for Jephthah, the first thing he sees on returning from battle is his daughter. He cannot break his vow to God, so he has to kill her.

Samson and the Philistines

FOR decades the Israelites had struggled with the warlike Philistines for control of the Promised Land. No matter how many defeats each nation suffered, they both refused to give up, and even though Barak and Deborah had previously crushed the entire Philistine army, the Philistines had slowly regained their strength. Now Israel once again fell into Philistine hands.

Yet God didn't entirely abandon the Israelites. He blessed a childless couple with a very special baby, Samson, sending an angel to tell them that one day he would stand up against the Philistines. The angel also warned the parents never to cut his hair.

Samson grew into a tall and exceptionally strong young man. But when he fell in love with a Philistine girl, his mother and father were utterly dismayed. They didn't know

that it was all part of God's plan, and they begged Samson to reconsider. But the wedding plans continued.

A grand wedding feast took place, with 30 Philistine guests of the bride invited. Everyone threw themselves into the celebrations and Samson decided to add to the fun by asking a riddle. He thought back to the time when he had been traveling to visit his bride-to-be and a lion had jumped out at him. The mighty Samson had killed the

Jaffa
This picture shows a view of Jaffa, on the Mediterranean coast of Israel. Today, it is part of the city of Tel Aviv, but in Old Testament times, it was part of Philistia (the land of the Philistines). In the Bible, it is called Joppa.

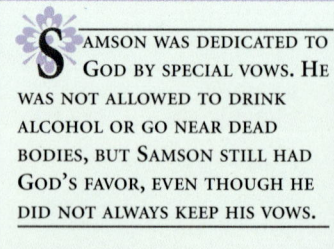

SAMSON WAS DEDICATED TO GOD BY SPECIAL VOWS. HE WAS NOT ALLOWED TO DRINK ALCOHOL OR GO NEAR DEAD BODIES, BUT SAMSON STILL HAD GOD'S FAVOR, EVEN THOUGH HE DID NOT ALWAYS KEEP HIS VOWS.

The Philistines
On the left is a Philistine warrior's coffin. The Philistines were the Israelites' greatest enemies. According to the Bible, they came from the Greek island of Crete and settled on the southern coastal plain of Canaan in the 12th century B.C. The Philistines had five main cities, each with its own ruler. The country of Palestine takes its name from the Philistines.

surprised lion with his bare hands. Later, on his return, Samson had seen that a swarm of bees had made a hive in the lion's carcass, and without fear he had reached in and taken a piece of the delicious honeycomb. These events made a nicely perplexing riddle:

"Out of the eater came something to eat,
Out of the strong came something sweet."

"Solve it by the end of the week," Samson challenged the Philistines, "and I will give each of you a set of fine clothes. If you fail, you must buy me rich clothes instead."

For days the guests racked their brains, until they were almost driven mad. As the baffled Philistines ran out of ideas, they decided to cheat. They went to the bride and told her that her life depended on telling them the secret.

Samson's young bride was so scared that she plagued her husband desperately for the answer to the riddle. On the seventh day, when she broke down and wept, Samson gave in. And before the sun went down, the Philistines had their answer.

> " *The Spirit of the Lord came mightily upon him and the ropes became as flax.* "

When Samson realized that he had been tricked by his guests he was furious. He stormed over to the nearest Philistine town and killed 30 citizens. He took the clothes that they were wearing, and he gave them to the Philistine wedding guests to keep his side of the bargain. Then, brokenhearted, he returned all alone to his father's house.

The Philistines turned on his sweetheart and her father and burned them inside their house. Samson was grief-stricken. "I swear I shall not stop until I have taken my vengeance on the whole nation," he vowed solemnly. But first he had to deal with the lynch mob who had arrived looking for him. Cunningly, he allowed the Israelites to tie his hands and lead him to his captors. There he broke free and seized a large jawbone that was lying at his feet. He attacked the Philistines in a frenzy, and by the time he stopped, he had killed 1,000 of his greatest enemies single-handed.

The Philistines didn't give up trying to catch Samson. When they found him sleeping one night, he escaped by simply lifting the city gates and walking away with them! It seemed as if it would never be possible to conquer the man with the strength of the Lord Himself.

Chosen by God
Samson was singled out by God from birth as special, so could ask God to perform a miracle and supply water to quench his thirst in the desert at Lehi.

Samson the Nazirite
Samson was a Nazirite—one who is dedicated to the service of God by special vows. Nazirites were not allowed to drink alcohol or to eat raisins or vinegar. They were forbidden from cutting their hair, and they had to avoid going near dead bodies. As the episode with the lion shows, Samson did not take his Nazirite vows very seriously.

❧ ABOUT THE STORY ❧

The Israelites have fallen under the rule of the Philistines. God sends a savior in the form of a baby boy. As a young man, Samson disappoints his parents by marrying a Philistine girl, but this is part of God's plan for him, and the alliance is short-lived. Samson is furious that he has been tricked into revealing the riddle about the lion, and he takes revenge. This is the first of Samson's personal battles against the Philistines.

Samson and Delilah

NEWS of Samson's feats of strength against the hated Philistines spread like wildfire through Israel, and the people's hero found himself made a Judge. This only inflamed the Philistines' hatred further, and they put Samson even higher on their "wanted" list.

While the Philistine leaders plotted and schemed, Samson fell in love with a girl named Delilah. But Samson hadn't learned his lesson. Like his former wife, Delilah was a Philistine. And unknown to him, she was soon bribed by Philistine chieftains to use her charms to get Samson to reveal the secret of his strength. She was completely snared by the promise of enough silver to make her very rich, and she did all she could to captivate the great

Israelite Judge. Often when they were alone together Delilah would cuddle up to Samson and ask, "Why won't you tell me how someone could take away your power?" Her innocent eyes and frustrated, inquiring tone gave her a childish air, and Samson never dreamed that Delilah was a cunning woman intent on deceiving him. She nudged and nagged, coaxed and cajoled, until Samson was forced to tell her something just to keep the peace! But he decided to have a little fun, and tease her for a while.

Little did Samson know that he was playing very dangerous games indeed. "If I am tied with seven new bowstrings, I will lose all my strength," he whispered to Delilah, with no idea that Philistine soldiers were hiding in the very next room. "Let me try, just for fun," begged Delilah, and bound him as tightly as she could. Then she stood back and put Samson to the test, crying out, "The Philistines are coming!" and daring him to break free. Imagine the disappointment on Delilah's face when the laughing Samson snapped out of his bowstrings as if they were cotton threads. "You fibbed!" she cried, stamping her foot. "Please tell me the real secret of your strength!"

"All right, all right," Samson shrugged. "If I'm bound with new, unused ropes, all my strength will leave me." Delilah clapped her hands with glee and rushed to tie him just as he had instructed. Yet once more Samson burst free, and the Philistine ambush stayed where they were.

"You're just mocking me," Delilah pouted. "Stop fooling around, now, and tell me the truth."

Samson pretended to be serious. "Take the seven braids of my hair and weave them into your loom, then you'll find my strength will fade." Very carefully, Delilah did as

Samson and Hercules
This picture shows a statue of the head of Hercules. In Greek and Roman mythology, Hercules was a hero of incredible strength and courage who performed 12 difficult tasks, or labors. After his death, he was made a god. In general, the word "Hercules" is used to mean a man of exceptional strength.

Parallels have been drawn between Samson, the strong man of the Bible, and Hercules, the strong man of Roman myth, comparing Samson's many feats of strength with Hercules' labors. However, while Hercules is a mythological character, there is strong historical evidence for Samson's existence. His birth and death are carefully documented, and the story of Samson as told in the Bible is closely connected with known historical events.

Dagon
Dagon was one of the main Philistine gods. He is often depicted as a fish god, but this is believed to be because of a confusion with the Hebrew word *dag* which means "fish." Another Hebrew word, *dagan,* means "grain," and it is possible that Dagon was a vegetation or grain god. He was first worshiped in Mesopotamia from at least 2500 B.C. onward.

> *'If I be shaved then my
> strength will leave me and I
> shall become weak.'*

she was told. But when she was finished and had made the weaving secure, Samson simply broke the loom with a flick of his head, enjoying the joke more than ever.

"How can you say you love me when you tell me nothing but lies!" Delilah sobbed. She sulked for weeks, making life so awful for Samson that in the end he could bear it no longer.

"If my hair is cut, I shall be like any other man," he confided. And Delilah knew he was telling the truth.

This time Delilah planned everything down to the last detail, so nothing could go wrong. She was so confident of success that she sent messages to the chieftains to come and collect Samson—bringing her money, of course—before she'd even taken him prisoner. First, she soothed Samson to sleep in her lap. Then, when he was snoring soundly, she gave the signal for a servant to creep in and cut off his precious long braids. Finally, with a small self-satisfied smile, she breathed in his ear to wake him. "Samson! Samson!" she whispered. "The Philistines are really coming!" Without realizing that his hair was gone, Samson sprang up to face the soldiers. But the strength of the Spirit of the Lord had indeed left him, and he was soon overpowered. As Samson stood before the Philistines in chains—knowing helplessness for the first time in his life—the cruel, merciless warriors blinded him by gouging out his eyes. Then, rejoicing at the great Israelite leader's misery, they flung him into the jail at Gaza.

Betrayed by Delilah
The name Delilah means "flirt," and the word has come to mean "a temptress." Delilah's greed for money leads her to collaborate with the Philistines and to betray Samson.

⚜ ABOUT THE STORY ⚜

Samson is persuaded by Delilah's charms to reveal the secret of his strength. When Samson's hair is cut, one of his Nazirite vows is broken. Until now, this was a vow he had kept. The vow is a sign of his dedication to God. Though Samson is physically strong, he is morally weak. His weakness symbolizes the weakness of all the Israelites, who have repeatedly broken God's laws and turned to other gods.

Destruction of the Temple

IN the double darkness of the prison dungeons and his blindness, Samson was put to work grinding grain, which hurt him at every move because of the shackles around his wrists and ankles. He had no family with him, no friends, and no possessions—only God and time. And as time passed, Samson's hair began to grow again without his even realizing.

The day came when the Philistines held an important festival in praise of their god, Dagon. Every man, woman and child was out in the streets to watch the sacrifices and join in the rejoicing, and this particular year the celebrations were better than ever. The Philistines had something really special to thank Dagon for, and they were determined to throw a party to remember. For Dagon had delivered into their hands the powerful Israelite leader who had single-handedly been the cause of thousands of Philistine deaths.

The merrymaking went on and on, and the worshipers grew wilder and wilder. Voices began to call for the famous prisoner to be brought up out of the jail and paraded for all the Philistines to see, so they could enjoy mocking and jeering at him to their hearts' content. Then the word went around that Samson was to be displayed in the temple itself, and the size of the crowds swelled immediately. How the Philistines longed to look down on their once dreaded enemy and sneer at him and show him in person just how much they hated him!

As soon as the first people caught sight of the wretched, blind Samson shuffling into the temple, they began to yell insults and ridicule him, and soon the noise and excitement was at fever pitch. The Philistine chieftains ordered Samson to be positioned right in the middle of the temple floor, between the two main supporting pillars, in order to give as many of their subjects as possible a good view. And the Israelite champion stood there as he

> **Strengthen me, I pray, this once that I may be avenged upon the Philistines.**

was told, quite broken and slumped, trying to block out the insults and obscenities that came hurtling through the darkness to his ears.

But as if from nowhere, a small spark of an idea suddenly began to glimmer in the blackness that now floated permanently before Samson. Slowly he bent down to the boy who was there to lead him around, and said, "Will you help me feel where the pillars are, so I can lean on them." Samson felt the lad take his hands and guide them out onto the cool rock on either side of him. Then silently Samson called out to the Lord with all the passion that was inside him. "O Lord, God, remember me, I pray," he beseeched, as he stood all on his own in the midst of his enemies. "I pray to you, O God, please give me my strength back just one more time—so I can be avenged

Samson's story
This picture of Samson dates from the 13th century. This means that it is not a realistic painting, but could tell the story of Samson to people at the time who could not read.

Grinding grain
Grinding grain would have been humiliating for Samson, as it was a job normally done by slaves. Samson, though, was probably put to work at a large mill, usually worked by oxen.

upon these people for the loss of my eyes." And Samson drew himself up and braced himself against the pillars, suddenly feeling the Spirit of the Lord flooding as strongly through his body as ever.

"Let me die with the Philistines!" he cried out, and heaved with all his might.

Not one of the Philistines had been able to hear above their own commotion what Samson had said. Yet they had seen him open his mouth and cry to Heaven, and had watched with mounting horror as the crushed, dejected prisoner had straightened up into a broad-shouldered warrior. Now their scornful cries of derision at once changed to howls and screams of terror as the pillars began to tremble and dust came crumbling down upon them from the ceiling. Before anyone could flee, Samson broke the pillars with an almighty crack, and the roof and walls of the huge temple came crashing inward, burying the thousands of people inside under tons of rubble.

That day, the mighty Samson died along with the Philistines. But he killed more enemies by dying than he had killed during all his life.

⚜ ABOUT THE STORY ⚜

Samson appears to be a broken man, but his faith is still strong, and God answers his prayer. Through Samson, God finally releases the Israelites from Philistine rule. Samson's destruction of the temple is symbolic of the Israelites' defeat of the Philistines.

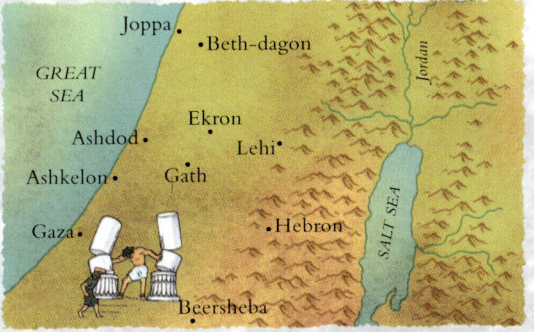

Samson
This map shows the area of Samson's war with the Philistines. It shows Lehi, where he killed the Philistines with the jawbone. You can also see Gaza, from where he took the city gates, and Hebron, where he left them. Finally, the Temple of Dagon, which he destroyed as he died, is at Gaza.

The Book of Ruth

DURING the days when the Judges ruled Israel, there was once a great famine that struck the land. Many people were forced either to leave their homes and settle elsewhere or to stay and starve. One man who chose to take his family away to safety was Elimelech. With his wife, Naomi, and his two sons, he went to live in Moab, where the crops were much more plentiful. There they were very happy at first, both boys taking Moabite wives: one named Orpah and the other Ruth. But in the space of ten years, all three men died, leaving their widows sad and lonely. Naomi longed to return to Israel, and made up her mind to go back. The brave widow talked to Orpah and Ruth about her difficult decision. "I consider you both my own daughters, but I shall go back to Israel by myself," she told the two young women. "There's no need for you to come too. You both belong here with your own people." Orpah and Ruth were devastated, but Naomi was insistent. Finally, sobbing with grief, Orpah agreed to remain in

> *'Where you go, I will go, your people shall be my people and your God, my God.'*

Moab. Ruth, however, flatly refused. "Wherever you go, I will go," she told Naomi, determinedly. "Your people will be my people, and your God my God. Only death itself will keep me from your side." So the two women set out on the long journey to Naomi's home town of Bethlehem.

They arrived at Bethlehem in the middle of the harvest, so Ruth managed to find work right away. As was the custom, she went with the other women of the city into the fields to gather the barley that the reapers had left behind. Ruth worked hard from morning until sunset. Her efforts were noticed by a landowner named Boaz, who asked his reapers who the young woman was. When Boaz heard that Ruth was Moabite and discovered how faithful she had been to her mother-in-law, he summoned Ruth to see him. "Stay in my fields, under my protection," he told her. "Whenever you get thirsty, help yourself to the water drawn for my reapers."

Ruth was quite overcome with his generosity. "Thank you," she blushed, quite embarrassed by the special treatment. "But why are you being so kind to me?"

Boaz smiled and told her gently that he had heard all about her kindness to Naomi. "May God reward you well for all that you have done," he praised her.

Later on, when the harvesters stopped to eat, Boaz not only called Ruth to come and join them but also gave her more than enough food. The young woman could hardly believe her good luck and hurried back to her work.

"Where on earth have you been working?" marveled Naomi when she saw the huge sack of grain and the large bundle of food her daughter-in-law had brought home.

ABOUT THE STORY

Although the Israelites have been turning away from God, this story illustrates how, for many individuals, faith in Him remains strong. It also shows that God is just as concerned with the lives of ordinary people as He is with the affairs of great leaders. Ruth discovers her new faith through her love for her mother-in-law. She goes on to produce a son who will become the grandfather of David, the first King of Israel.

Everyday life
The picture shows Ruth working in the fields. While this story relates to the same period as the stories of the Judges before it, its tone and content are very different. It deals with ordinary life, which would have been relevant to many people of the time. Most people during the period of the Judges still had to make a living from the land.

Meeting place
Business deals often took place at the town gates, like the gates of Damascus shown here, since there were plenty of people around to act as witnesses. Boaz was not Ruth's nearest male relative, so he had to meet the man who was called a "kinsman-redeemer" and buy the right to acquire Naomi's land and marry Ruth. The kinsman-redeemer gave his sandal to Boaz as a sign of the agreement.

"The landowner's name is Boaz," she began, but could get no further before Naomi interrupted her.

"Boaz?" the widow cried, her face lighting up with excitement. "Boaz is one of my dead husband's closest relatives! This has to be the Lord's work! Thanks to God!" And the two women's hearts were filled with gladness.

When the harvest was over Ruth found herself out of work.

"We'll have to tell Boaz that we're family, and maybe he will take pity on us," Naomi told her. Ruth put on her finest clothes and went off to find Boaz.

Boaz was sleeping by his grain to protect it when Ruth arrived. She silently went to the end of his sleeping mat and covered herself with the corner of Boaz's robe. When Boaz woke, he was deeply moved by Ruth's plea. "I will do everything in my power to look after you," he said.

The next day, Boaz formally took Ruth and her mother-in-law under his protection. He met Ruth's "kinsman-redeemer," Naomi's nearest living male relative, and bought the right to marry her, sealing the deal, as was customary, by receiving his sandal.

Boaz cared for Ruth and Naomi from that day onward. He married Ruth, and in due course she gave birth to their son, Obed, who was to become the grandfather of David, the greatest of all the Israelite kings.

Ruth and Naomi
Ruth decided to make the long journey with Naomi to Bethlehem. Although she thought that she was giving up the chance to remarry and settle down, her first loyalty was to Naomi. She was still rewarded, though, by her marriage to Boaz, and the birth of their child.

Threshing and winnowing
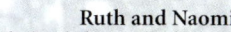
After the barley had been harvested, it was beaten with a threshing board, then winnowed—tossed into the air with a fork so that the grain separated from the stalks. The light stalks blew away, while the heavy grain fell straight to the floor.

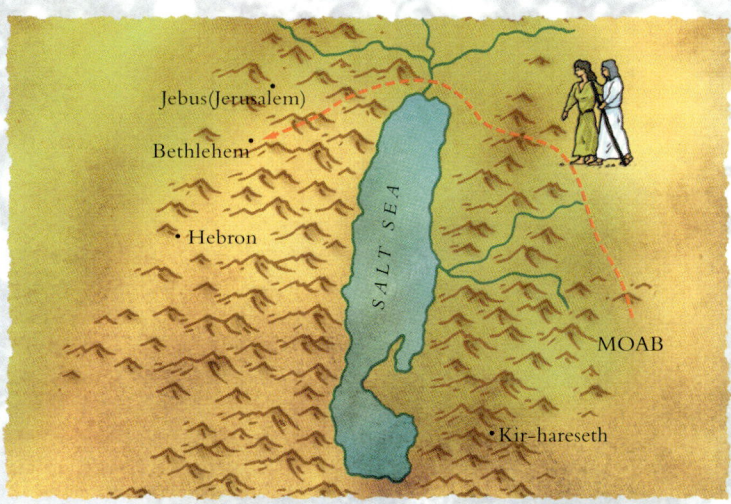

Jebus(Jerusalem)

Bethlehem

Hebron

SALT SEA

MOAB

Kir-hareseth

Moses

MOSES is one of the great leaders in the Bible. His life was eventful from the very start. Desperate to save her baby son from the Pharaoh's decree that all Hebrew male babies should be killed, Moses' mother put him into a reed basket and hid him among the bulrushes that grew beside the Nile. Found by one of Pharaoh's daughters, he was brought up by her at the royal court.

As a young man, Moses felt sympathy for his fellow-Israelites, who were often ill-treated by their Egyptian masters. When he witnessed an Egyptian overseer beating an Israelite slave, he was so angry, he killed the man. The news reached Pharaoh's ears and Moses fled to safety outside Egypt's borders. During this time, he received a sign from God, in the form of a burning bush, telling him that he was to become the savior of the Israelite people.

After battling against a great deal of opposition from Pharaoh, Moses finally succeeded in leading his people out of Egypt, to search for the land God had promised them. On Mount Sinai, Moses spoke directly with God and received the Ten Commandments and other laws.

During the 40 years of exile in the wilderness, Moses remained loyal to his people and to his God. Despite the Israelites' regular lapses of faith in God and their rebellions against Moses' own leadership, he stood by them, frequently pleading to God for mercy on their behalf. When Moses' own sister, Miriam, complained about him, claiming that God had spoken to her as well as to Moses, God rebuked her, explaining that although he appeared to other people in visions or dreams, the way in which he appeared to Moses was different. He said, "With him will I speak mouth to mouth, even clearly, and not in dark speeches" (Numbers 12:8).

Although he devoted his whole life to God, Moses was not above sin himself. On one occasion, in the wilderness, he used his rod to bring forth water from a rock, instead of just speaking to the rock, as God had ordered. For this disobedience, he was forbidden entry into the Promised Land, though he did climb Mount Nebo to view it from a distance, shortly before his death.

A man of God
Throughout his life, Moses' faith in God never wavered. He was a trusting and obedient servant until the day he died. Despite all his achievements, and his status as God's chosen one, he remained meek, humble, and patient, always putting his people's needs before his own. He was both a great man and a great leader.

The death of Moses
The book of Deuteronomy describes the death of Moses, finishing with the following words about one of the greatest of Old Testament prophets. "And there has not arisen in Israel a prophet since like Moses, whom the Lord knew face to face, none like him for all the signs and wonders which the Lord sent him to do in the land of Egypt, to Pharaoh and to all his servants and to all his land, and for all the mighty power and all the great and terrible deeds which Moses wrought in the sight of all Israel."

Deuteronomy 34:10–12.

The Battle of Beliefs

ON their arrival in the land of Canaan, the Israelites fought many battles with the local people, in an attempt to take over their land. Alongside the war over land, another war was also being fought—a war of religion.

God had instructed the Israelites to drive the Canaanites away from their lands. He knew that the local people worshiped different gods, and that their religion might influence the Israelites. At first, the Israelites obeyed God, but as the years went by, they grew tired of constantly fighting the Canaanites and began to live alongside them as neighbors. As God had predicted, they also began to worship their gods.

Statue worship
Many Israelites were attracted to the Canaanite gods because they could worship statues, which was forbidden by their own God.

Destroying the altar
Gideon destroyed his father's altar to Baal and built a new altar to God. He went on to defeat the hordes of invading Midianites with an army of only 300 men.

Gideon and the angel
In this picture, the angel of the Lord commands Gideon to destroy his father's altar to Baal, together with its statue. Gideon was appointed by God as one of the Judges who would save the Israelites from their enemies.

One aspect of Canaanite religion that the Israelites would have liked was the idea of worshiping an image, such as a statue, of a god or goddess. It would have been far more satisfying to worship something they could actually see, as the Israelites were forbidden to worship idols by Moses' second commandment.

The other reason the Israelites turned to the local gods was these gods' apparent control over the fertility of the land. Once the Israelites settled down to become farmers, their crops were very important to them. Many of the Canaanite gods were linked to nature and fertility, and, because of this, they seemed to the Israelites to have more direct influence over their daily life than their God. The Canaanites were very successful farmers; some took this as evidence of the superiority of Baal.

Canaanite gods
These are three of the main Canaanite gods. Dagon is believed to be a god of grain or vegetation. Baal, is a weather god associated with thunderstorms and rain. He is often shown holding a bolt of lightning. Asherah is a fertility goddess associated with Baal.

DAGON   BAAL   ASHERAH

Battling on
While the physical battles of clashing swords and shields raged noisily around Canaan, the quieter battle of beliefs was also going on.

The Judges

THE officials called Judges were originally appointed by Moses during the wilderness years. His father-in-law, Jethro, suggested that they could take some of the burden of responsibility from Moses's shoulders. These were Judges in the legal sense, in the way that people use the word today. After the death of Joshua, no single leader took over, and the Judges took on the role of rulers in peacetime and military leaders in wartime. So the word "judge" came to mean "leader" or "governor."

Ehud and Eglon
Ehud was one of the early Judges. He saved the Israelites from the Moabites by killing their king, Eglon.

Deborah's wisdom
Deborah used to sit under a palm tree and hand out advice to Israelites who came to her for help with settling their disputes.

The Book of Judges in the Old Testament tells of the lives of these Judges. Their main role was to save the Israelite people from their enemies and to try and keep them faithful to God's laws. During the time of the Judges, a pattern of events kept repeating itself. The Israelites turned away from God and started to worship the Canaanite gods, so God punished them by letting them fall into the hands of a foreign ruler. The people repented and promised to change their ways, so God appointed a Judge to save them. For a period of time, the people mended their ways, but after the death of the Judge, they slipped back into their sinful habits.

There were 14 Judges, the first being Othniel and the last Samuel. Some ruled for a very short time and achieved nothing of great importance. Others were more significant. One of these was Deborah, a woman Judge who, together with Barak, saved the Israelites from the Canaanite General Sisera. Gideon took on the mighty army of the Midianites with a force of only 300 men. Another Judge was Jephthah, a brigand who defeated the Ammonites. The most famous Judge is Samson, who made many attacks on the Philistines. Under Samuel, the last Judge, and under the first Kings, the nation of Israel was eventually brought together, and the Philistines were finally defeated.

TIMELINE 1400 B.C. TO 1000 B.C.

• Moses receives the Ten Commandments, but finds the people worshiping the golden calf so he smashes the tablets.

1400 B.C.   MOSES SMASHES THE STONE TABLETS

THE ISRAELITES CROSS THE RIVER JORDAN

• Moses, Israel's greatest leader, dies.

• Joshua is appointed leader of the Israelites.

• Joshua takes the Israelites across the River Jordan into Canaan, and leads them in victory against Jericho.

1300 B.C.   120

Samson and the Nazirite Laws

THE Judges were chosen by God to lead and judge his people. It is confusing, therefore, to see that some of these appointed leaders, who were held up as examples to their people, lived their own lives in a way that was far from what people might expect and seemed to disregard many of God's laws.

The most obvious example is Samson. He was a Nazirite, which meant that he was dedicated from birth to the service of God by special vows. Nazirites were not allowed to cut their hair or to come into contact with dead bodies. Samson broke most of his Nazirite vows, by allowing Delilah to cut off his hair, and by eating honey from the carcass of a lion he had killed.

Although it is hard to accept the behavior of Judges like Samson in positions of authority, we must remember that all the Judges are instruments of God, and their actions are part of God's plan. For example, it is because Samson allows Delilah to cut his hair that he is captured by the Philistines. In their temple God gives him back his strength so he can kill several thousand of them at once. God's purpose for Samson is to defeat the Philistines, so He allows some of His laws to be broken in order to achieve something more important.

Forbidden food
Samson broke his Nazirite vows by eating honey from a nest bees had made in a lion's carcass.

The strongest man
When Samson was found in Gaza, he escaped by uprooting the city gates and walking away with them.

Tricked by a woman
Delilah tricked Samson into revealing the secret of his strength and then betrayed him to the Philistines.

• Joshua renews the Israelites' covenant with God before he dies.

ISRAELITES' WEAPONS AND A SHEKEL

• After the death of Joshua, the Israelites lose their faith in God. They begin to worship Canaanite idols, and fall into the hands of Canaanite rulers.

• Deborah and Barak rescue the Israelites from the army of Sisera.

• Gideon rescues the Israelites from the Midianites.

DEBORAH DEFEATS SISERA

JEPHTHAH'S DAUGHTER

• Jephthah defeats the invading Ammonites, but pays for his foolish vow to God when he returns home.

1100 B.C.

• Samson the Nazirite judges Israel and defeats the Philistines.

• Ruth and Naomi make their journey to Bethlehem. Ruth marries Boaz, and Obed is born.

PHILISTINE WARRIOR'S COFFIN

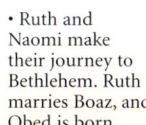

1000 B.C.

Glossary

altar of witness
An altar, a replica of the altar in the tabernacle at Shiloh, built by the tribes of Reuben, Gad and Manasseh to bear witness to future generations of all the tribes the fact that even though they were separated from the rest of the tribes of Israel by the River Jordan, they all still worshiped the same God.

Ark
The Ark of the Covenant, also called the Ark of the Testimony, is a box made of acacia wood, inlaid with gold, with two cherubim on top. It was built to hold the stone tablets of the Ten Commandments, but also later held the pot of manna, Aaron's rod and the written law. It was the symbol of God's presence among his people and played an important role in the fall of Jericho. The Israelites also carried the Ark before them as they crossed the River Jordan to show that God was leading them to the Promised Land.

Asherah
A Caananite goddess, worshiped at the time that the Israelites were invading Canaan. She was worshiped as an Asherah pole, a figure carved from a piece of wood, very often a complete tree trunk. Gideon the Judge was asked by the angel to detroy his father's Baal statue and Asherah pole.

astrology
This is a way that people believed that they could tell the future, by looking at the stars and planets and their position in the sky (see diviner).

Baal
Baal was the main god of the Canaanites at this time. He was a fertility god: the people believed that he made the crops grow for them. He was also a thunder god, and he is often pictured holding or throwing a bolt of lightning.

Commandments
The Ten Commandments were the most important of the laws that God gave to Moses on Mount Sinai. They are addressed to the whole of the Israelite nation and to everyone as an individual. They were the terms of the covenant between God and his people and were produced on two stone tablets. This probably means that there were two copies—at this time when a covenant or agreement was made between two people or two countries, they took a copy each so they both knew what they had to do, just as you would with a contract today.

Dagon
Dagon is the main God of the Philistines. He is often represented as a fish god, but it is more likely that he was a god of grain or wheat.

diviner
Balaam was a diviner, someone who believes that they can tell the future by looking at different everyday objects. Divining was forbidden by Moses, but people continued to practice various methods (see astrology, rhabdomancy).

Holy of Holies
This is the very center of the tabernacle, where the Ark of the Covenant is kept.

idol/idolatry
An idol is a statue of a person, god, or animal, and idolatry is worshiping the statue, which is forbidden to the Israelites in the Ten Commandments. The Canaanites were idolatrous, as they worshiped statues of their gods, Baal, Asherah and Dagon. It was easier for the Israelites to worship something that they could actually see, which is why some of them found it so difficult to resist the Canaanite religions. For this reason, God told the Israelites they must destroy all other religions as they conquered the Promised Land, because they would be drawn into worshiping idols.

manna
This is the substance that was the main food of the Israelites while they were in the desert. The Bible says that after the dew had gone there was found on the ground a "small round thing," whitish, like coriander seed, and with a honey taste. The Israelites used it in cooking.

miracle
Miracles are acts perfomed by God, either Himself, or acting through someone, such as Moses. They not only show God's power, but they also form part of how God reveals Himself to His creation, humans.

Nazirite
A Nazirite is someone who is dedicated to the service of God by special vows. Nazirites were not allowed to drink alcohol, or to eat raisins or vinegar. They were forbidden from cutting their hair, and they had to avoid going near dead bodies.

rhabdomancy
This is a way that people believed that they could tell the future, throwing arrow heads into the air and reading the future from the way that they landed (see diviner).

tabernacle
The tabernacle, or "tent of meeting," was the focus for the Israelites' worship of God while they were in the desert. The Ark was put into the central room of the tabernacle, and a cloud descended and a bright light shone from the tent, showing that God had taken up residence among His people.

Index

Page numbers in **bold** refer to illustrations.

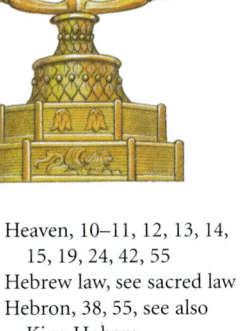